DON WEEKES

RED-HOT
HOCKEY
TRIVIA

GREY$TONE BOOKS
Douglas & McIntyre Publishing Group
Vancouver/Toronto/Berkeley

For Camil Desroches

Greystone Books
A division of Douglas & McIntyre Ltd.
2323 Quebec Street, Suite 201
Vancouver, British Columbia
Canada V5T 4S7
www.greystonebooks.com

NATIONAL LIBRARY OF CANADA CATALOGUING IN PUBLICATION DATA
Weekes, Don
  Red-hot hockey trivia/Don Weekes.

  ISBN-13: 978-1-55054-843-3   ISBN-10: 1-55054-843-3
  1. National Hockey League—Miscellanea. 2. Hockey—Miscellanea. I. Title.
GV847.W434 2003   796.962'64   C2003-910888-0

Library of Congress information is available upon request.

Editing by Christine Kondo
Cover design by Jessica Sullivan
Cover photograph by Bruce Bennett Studios
Typeset by Tanya Lloyd Kyi
Printed and bound in Canada by Friesens
Distributed in the U.S. by Publishers Group West

We gratefully acknowledge the financial support of the Canada Council for the Arts, the British Columbia Arts Council, and the Government of Canada through the Book Publishing Industry Development Program (BPIDP) for our publishing activities

Don Weekes *is an award-winning television producer-director at* CTV *in Montreal. He has written 20 hockey trivia books. He is the co-author of* The Unofficial Guide to Hockey's Most Unusual Records.

CONTENTS

PREFACE

The hockey gods must have a soft spot for trivia.

While the NHL free falls into the defensive systems of the trap and left-wing lock, declining attendance, flat television ratings and bankruptcy court (for its failing franchises), the league never fails to deliver great hockey trivia. Somehow every season is loaded with record breakers and chart toppers that give fans new heroes to cheer and a few zeroes to smear.

The 2002–03 NHL season was especially rewarding. A new record was set for the two fastest goals from the start of a game, the lowest goals-against average in modern-day hockey was established and one team recorded the longest stretch ever of one-goal victories. Then, for the first time, a pile of players were publicly tarred and feathered for diving infractions. Were they disgraced? About as much as the veteran defenseman whose fans nicknamed "Breeze-by."

New trivia gems unearthed from past seasons proved just as entertaining, such as the only rearguard to lead all members of his team in goal scoring in one season; the rookie with the fastest assist from a career start; the only 42-year-olds to get as many points as their age; the last blueliner honoured with the Lady Byng Trophy as the league's most gentlemanly player.

Outside the NHL, the spirit of hockey lived on in 2002–03 with a few stories that are bound to become legend in our game. In Alberta, a group of 40 amateur players established a new record for the world's longest hockey game. Next door, a Saskatchewan community made national headlines with a "guess-when-the-rusted-Chevy-sinks-through-the-ice" contest to raise money to save its local rink. And far from home, Hayley Wickenheiser became the first woman to score a goal in a men's pro league in Finland.

In this our twentieth trivia book, we champion the red-hot warriors of hockey who, despite the defensive strategies of their coaches, have never lacked the character to get it all done.

By the way, why have we waited so long for a left-winger to win the NHL scoring title? And what is the cost of a first-rate customized back-yard rink? Let's see the hockey gods stickhandle some answers around those queries.

DON WEEKES
May 2003

1
HARVEY THE HOUND

After being taunted by Calgary Flames mascot Harvey the Hound from behind a glass partition during a game in January 2003, Edmonton coach Craig MacTavish grabbed Harvey's 30-centimetre red tongue, tore it out and threw it into the crowd. Harvey continued to goad the coach, who then threatened the Flames' mascot with a stick. In Canada, the story was front-page news. In this opening chapter on general hockey trivia we rip a few other stories from the headlines.

(Answers are on page 6)

1.1 Which NHLer has played in the most regular-season wins during his career?
A. Ray Bourque
B. Scott Stevens
C. Mark Messier
D. Larry Robinson

1.2 Nashville's Jordin Tootoo is the first NHL prospect from what race of people?
A. Tootoo is an American Aboriginal
B. Tootoo is a Polynesian
C. Tootoo is an Australian Aborigine
D. Tootoo is a Canadian Inuit

1.3 Which 1960s player first made waving to the crowd at centre ice popular after receiving a star of the game?
A. Jean Béliveau
B. Johnny Bower
C. Eddie Shack
D. Gump Worsley

1.4 When Dany Heatley scored four goals at the 2003 All-Star Game he unseated Wayne Gretzky as the youngest All-Star to score a hat trick. How much younger was Heatley than Gretzky?
A. One day
B. One week
C. One month
D. One year

1.5 In February 2003 a group of 40 amateur players from Alberta set a new record for the world's longest hockey game. How long did they play?
A. 40 hours
B. 60 hours
C. 80 hours
D. 100 hours

1.6 Who finally overtook Mike Gartner as the NHL's fastest skater?
A. Saku Koivu of the Montreal Canadiens
B. Sergei Zubov of the Dallas Stars
C. Jason Chimera of the Edmonton Oilers
D. Marian Gaborik of the Minnesota Wild

1.7 When Canadian-born Hayley Wickenheiser joined the Kirkkonummi Lightning of the Finnish league in 2002–03, she became the second woman to play in a men's pro league. How many games did she play before she scored her first goal?
A. Wickenheiser never scored a goal in 2002–03
B. One game
C. Three games
D. Six games

1.8 What is the greatest number of NHL teams one player has been acquired by without playing a single NHL game?
A. Two teams
B. Three teams

C. Four teams

D. Five teams

1.9 Who is Tim Hurlbut?

A. A Calgary streaker

B. The Zamboni driver at Toronto's Air Canada Centre

C. A controversial Vancouver radio host

D. The new owner of the Buffalo Sabres

1.10 Which elite NHLer is a *Stars Wars* fanatic?

A. Peter Forsberg

B. Paul Kariya

C. Jaromir Jagr

D. Dany Heatley

1.11 How many games did it take Cliff Ronning before he scored his first empty-net goal?

A. Ronning has never scored an empty netter

B. 100 games

C. 500 games

D. More than 1,000 games

1.12 What is the greatest number of career games played by an NHLer who was drafted and then traded in the same summer?

A. 64 games

B. 364 games

C. 664 games

D. 964 games

1.13 What is the most number of times one player has been through successive expansion drafts?

A. No player has been through more than one expansion draft

B. Two straight expansion drafts

C. Three straight expansion drafts

D. Four straight expansion drafts

1.14 At the 2003 trade deadline a new record was set for most deals. How many transactions took place to break the old record of 20 deals in 1999?
A. 22 deals
B. 24 deals
C. 28 deals
D. 32 deals

1.15 As of 2002–03 how many sets of twins have been drafted into the NHL?
A. Two sets of twins
B. Four sets of twins
C. Six sets of twins
D. Eight sets of twins

1.16 Who are the first twins to play in the NHL?
A. Peter and Chris Ferraro
B. Ron and Rich Sutter
C. Patrik and Peter Sundstrom
D. Daniel and Henrik Sedin

1.17 In what year did a defenseman last win the Lady Byng Trophy as the league's most gentlemanly player?
A. 1953–54
B. 1963–64
C. 1973–74
D. 1983–84

1.18 What is the highest penalty-shot count by a player who failed to score a goal?
A. Three penalty shots
B. Four penalty shots
C. Five penalty shots
D. Six penalty shots

1.19 Which old timer was the first NHLer to score two penalty-shot goals in one season?
   A. Charlie Conacher of the Toronto Maple Leafs
   B. Sid Abel of the Detroit Red Wings
   C. Pat Egan of the Brooklyn Americans
   D. Maurice Richard of the Montreal Canadiens

1.20 Who was the first player to break one of Wayne Gretzky's 61 NHL records?
   A. Brett Hull
   B. Ray Bourque
   C. Joe Sakic
   D. Ron Francis

1.21 Who is Jay North?
   A. The first high school player drafted by an NHL team
   B. The first full-blooded Native NHL player
   C. The first NHLer assessed a fighting major
   D. The first goal-scoring leader not elected an All-Star

1.22 Who won the face-off that led to Mario Lemieux scoring the winning goal in the 1987 Canada Cup?
   A. Wayne Gretzky
   B. Doug Gilmour
   C. Dale Hawerchuk
   D. Mark Messier

1.23 Bobby Orr is synonymous with No. 4, but the Bruins' great actually wanted another number when he joined Boston in 1966–67. Which number?
   A. No. 2
   B. No. 6
   C. No. 9
   D. No. 13

1.24 What is the highest sweater number worn by an NHLer since Wayne Gretzky retired?
- A. No. 95
- B. No. 96
- C. No. 97
- D. No. 98

HARVEY THE HOUND
Answers

1.1 B. Scott Stevens

Player performance is never evaluated on the number of team wins, but the statistics are fascinating. Stevens has been on the winning end of more regular-season games than anyone else in league history. Larry Robinson has the best winning percentage, a 59 per cent rate. The only forward among the top five in the team-wins category is Mark Messier.

MOST REGULAR-SEASON WINS BY A PLAYER

Player	Teams	GP	Team Wins
Scott Stevens	Wsh., St. L., N.J.	1,597	859
Mark Messier	Edm., NYR, Van.	1,680	840
Ray Bourque	Bos., Col.	1,612	832
Larry Robinson	Mtl., L.A.	1,384	815
Larry Murphy	L.A., Wsh., Min., Pit., Tor., Det.	1,615	814

Figures courtesy of *The Hockey News*. Current to 2002–03.

1.2 D. Tootoo is a Canadian Inuit

NHLers have come from every nook and cranny across Canada, but Tootoo is the first player of Inuit descent drafted into the NHL. It's a big surprise that the five-foot-eight winger even made it. And not because he's almost a half-foot shorter than the average NHLer. Tootoo didn't play organized hockey until he was 14 years old. In his hometown of Rankin Inlet on the northern shore of Hudson Bay, there weren't enough boys to ice more than one team at any age level. "I made history, I guess," said Tootoo after being selected 98th overall by the Nashville Predators in 2001.

1.3 B. Johnny Bower

Hockey's long-standing tradition of the three star selection and the skate to centre ice by those stars after the game took on an added twist when Johnny Bower began waving to fans each time he received a game star during the 1960s. Bower admitted the gesture was originally intended for his wife's mother, but later for all the grandmothers watching him play. On one occasion, after receiving a star which he felt undeserving of, Bower did not perform his usual wave. As a result, the Toronto netminder was flooded with letters from furious grannies, scolding him for not waving to them at centre ice.

1.4 A. One day

Heatley was 22 years, 12 days old when he potted his four All-Star goals in 2003, just one day younger than Gretzky, who had held the distinction of being the youngest All-Star to score a hat trick since 1983's All-Star contest. The 2001–02 rookie of the year recorded his first goal after stick-handling around Rob Blake and firing a low shot past Patrick Roy. "After I got the first one, I was pretty happy," Heatley said. "After that they kept going in. I kept cruising around and shooting the puck." On Heatley's second goal, he batted the puck out of midair to score, which drew praise from his victim. "I'd say the guy has a lot of talent to do that," said Roy. Heatley also scored in the first-ever All-Star shootout, but the goal, his fifth of the game, didn't count towards his totals in official scoring. Heatley was the 13th All-Star to score a hat trick and just one of five with a four-goal game. The Great One also scored four goals in 1983.

1.5 **C. 80 hours**

As soon as this 80-hour record was set on February 16, 2003, it became a target for other crazies to break, including the rink rats from Moosomin, Saskatchewan, the players who set the original mark at 62 hours 15 minutes. In the Alberta marathon, 40 friends played on an outdoor rink in hour-long shifts, taking breaks in a converted garage-turned-dressing room. A hot tub provided relief from muscle cramps over the four-day stretch. They played in full equipment under NHL rules with very little physical contact. The final score was 650–628 for the Blue team—not the defensive-style game of coach Jacques Lemaire—but the event did raise CDN$40,000 for cancer research.

1.6 **C. Jason Chimera of the Edmonton Oilers**

At the 2003 Oilers skills competition, rookie left-winger Jason Chimera turned a lap in 13.332 seconds to best right-winger Mike Gartner's record of 13.386 from the 1986 All-Star game.

1.7 **D. Six games**

Hayley Wickenheiser, star of Canada's national team and some-times known as the female Wayne Gretzky, scored her first goal in her sixth game with Kirkkonummi, a third-division semi-pro team from Finland. Despite her goal and an assist during the February 1, 2003 game, the Lightning lost 5–4. Wickenheiser is the first woman to score a goal in a men's pro hockey league.

1.8 **C. Four teams**

We expect this might be a record, if not, it's a good hockey story anyway. Since being chosen 34th overall by Tampa Bay in the 2000 Entry Draft, Ruslan Zainullin has been shipped to Phoenix, Atlanta and Calgary. Four teams and the 20-year-old centre from Kazan, Russia, has yet to play a single game as of 2002–03. "He's the most unheard of guy who's been traded three times. He must have a wall of sweaters in his house," said Oilers VP of hockey operations Kevin Prendergast.

1.9   A. A Calgary streaker

Few who saw the news footage will forget the story of Tim Hurlbut, the Calgary streaker who scaled the glass at the Saddledome during a Boston game on October 17, 2002, fell on the ice and was knocked out cold for six minutes while wearing only a pair of red socks. Hurlbut—a name befitting the man's actions—was intoxicated. An Alberta judge ordered Hurlbut to pay CDN$2,500 to two charities, do community service and chastised him for the "pathetic spectacle of yourself splayed naked on the ice for six minutes until you were covered." A few weeks later, a Calgary nightclub called Cowboys Dance Hall, planned a fundraiser for Hurlbut, the man "who brought so much joy into our lives with a simple pair of red socks."

1.10   B. Paul Kariya

In a *Hockey News* interview, Matt Cullen, Kariya's former roommate with the Mighty Ducks, revealed that his friend is obsessed with *Star Wars*. "It's kind of embarrassing to be honest with you. He'd always want to talk to me about *Star Wars* and I'd just sit back or just laugh and pretend I didn't hear him. He's just fanatic. It's sad, it's really, really pathetic, I think that is the word. Yea, he takes heat. Guys are all over him. He for sure has a nerdy side," said Cullen.

1.11   D. More than 1,000 games

Whatever game plan coaches use to protect a lead late in the game, it doesn't appear Ronning plays any part in it. Otherwise he should have had a few empty-netters before his 17th season. It came in Ronning's 1,080th game as Minnesota beat Montreal 6–3 on February 27, 2003. Because it felt so good, Ronning scored another one seven games later against Nashville. Coincidently, Ronning was promoted to full captain in March, a first in the right-winger's career.

1.12 **D. 964 games**
The most successful players drafted and traded in the same summer are Doug Jarvis and Bob Bourne. In one of hockey's most amazing coincidences, both Bourne and Jarvis played the exact same number of career games, 964 matches, won the exact same number of Stanley Cups exactly the same way, four straight Cups for their respective traded-to teams, and retired in the same season, 1987–88. Bourne was drafted 38th overall by Kansas City in 1974 before being traded in September to the New York Islanders. Jarvis, hockey's all-time ironman, was chosen 24th overall by Toronto and dealt to Montreal just weeks after the 1975 Entry Draft.

1.13 **C. Three straight expansion drafts**
Originally drafted 185th overall by the Washington Capitals in 1984, Jim Thomson was kicked around by three teams— Washington, Hartford and New Jersey—before arriving in Los Angeles where he was yo-yoed in league expansion drafts to Minnesota in 1991, Ottawa in 1992 and Anaheim in 1993. Clearly, Thomson was your borderline player. His best friend was league expansion.

1.14 **B. 24 deals**
A few new marks were set at the trade deadline on March 11, 2003. A record 46 players changed teams in a league-high 24 deals. Highlighting the day, Detroit picked up Mathieu Schneider from Los Angeles, Toronto got greybeards Phil Housley from Chicago and Doug Gilmour from Montreal and St. Louis shored up its crease with Chris Osgood from the Islanders.

1.15 **C. Six sets of twins**
Daniel and Henrik Sedin may be the NHL's most famous twins after being picked second and third overall by Vancouver in the 1999 Entry Draft, but they are only one of six sets of twin brothers drafted into the league. Patrik and Peter Sundstrom, the

first and only twins drafted in separate years, were selected in 1980 and 1981. Ron and Rich Sutter both went in the first round of 1982; Peter and Ray Ferraro were picked in the 1992 draft; and two set of twins were drafted in 2000: Matt and Mark McRae (both went to the Atlanta Thrashers) and Paul and Peter Flache.

1.16 B. Ron and Rich Sutter
The Sutters from Viking, Alberta, are hockey's most productive family, bearing six siblings of NHL caliber in one generation. Twins Ron and Rich were rookies in 1982–83. They snuck in just ahead of Patrik and Peter Sundstrom by a year. Patrik began in 1982–83 and Peter in 1983–84. The Sutter twins are also the first twins to play on the same team, Philadelphia in 1983–84.

1.17 A. 1953–54
Defenseman Nicklas Lidstrom might have been the best bet to break with a half-century tradition of Lady Byng winners from the forward ranks. But the Detroit rearguard finished runner-up three straight years—1999, 2000 and 2001—to keep Red Kelly's 1954 Lady Byng the last by a rearguard. Kelly was named most gentlemanly player three times: in 1950–51 (24 penalty minutes), in 1952–53 (eight minutes) and 1953–54 (18 minutes).

1.18 C. Five penalty shots
Vancouver's Greg Adams had a knack for earning penalty shots, he just couldn't capitalize on his one-on-one opportunities. Interestingly, all his shots came early in his 17-year career. After five consecutive misses he probably went out of his way to avoid further embarrassment. Adams played from 1984–85 to 2000–01.

1.19 C. Pat Egan of the Brooklyn Americans
Last-place Brooklyn piled up the losses in 1941–42, but they didn't get pushed around, not with rugged rearguard Pat Egan

and his league-leading 124 penalty minutes. Egan scored only eight goals, but 25 per cent came from two penalty-shot goals, one against Montreal's Bert Gardiner on November 16, 1941, and the other against Chicago's Sam LoPresti on March 5, 1942.

1.20 B. Ray Bourque
Few would have figured a defenseman to be the first to break one of Wayne Gretzky's 61 NHL scoring records. But that record-breaker was Ray Bourque, hockey's all-time leading point earner among rearguards. Bourque broke Gretzky's mark of 12 All-Star game assists on February 6, 2000, when he assisted on a goal by Tony Amonte at 12:14 of the second period at the 2000 All-Star game. Five minutes later Mark Messier also notched his 13th career assist on a Ray Whitney goal. The first player to break a Gretzky regular-season record was Adam Oates. Oates toppled the Great One's career record of 15 overtime assists in 2001–02 when he collected his 14th, 15th and 16th overtime helpers with the Capitals and Flyers.

1.21 A. The first high school player drafted by an NHL team
A number of famous high schoolers have gone directly from their school books to the NHL record books. Before Bobby Carpenter made history as the first player drafted directly from high school into the NHL in 1981, Jay North and seven other high schoolers were chosen in 1980. North, from Bloomington-Jefferson High School in Minnesota, was selected by Buffalo 62nd overall.

1.22 C. Dale Hawerchuk
Hawerchuk, who was inducted into the Hockey Hall of Fame in 2001, was a key performer at the 1987 Canada Cup. Although he was one of the NHL's top scorers, the Winnipeg Jets' star was asked to assume a checking role on the talent-laden Canadian squad, which he performed with great effectiveness. Coach Mike Keenan selected Hawerchuk to take the key face-off against Russia late in the third period of a 5–5 tie in the tournament's

decisive game. As Hawerchuk recalled at his Hall of Fame induction: "Mike sent me out there on a hunch. I was lucky enough to win the face-off, and a couple of seconds later—slip, slip—it's on Mario's stick and it's in the net and the country is going crazy."

1.23 A. No. 2
Orr wanted No. 2, the number he had worn during his junior career with the Oshawa Generals of the Ontario Hockey Association. But that digit had been retired in honour of Boston Bruins defenseman Eddie Shore. Orr was assigned No. 27 when he joined the Bruins in 1966–67, but when Al Langlois, who had been wearing No. 4, was cut from the team before the start of the season, Orr took his number because it was the closest to No. 2 that he could get.

1.24 C. No. 97
Since the Great One quit hockey in 1999 and his famous No. 99 was retired league-wide, the next highest jersey number donned by a player belongs to Philadelphia's Jeremy Roenick. He wore No. 27 in Chicago, but after his trade to Phoenix at the 1997 Entry Draft, Roenick picked No. 97. During 2002–03 there were less than a dozen players who sported sweater numbers in the nineties.

STANLEY'S MVP

Only one forward in NHL history has captured the Conn Smythe Trophy as playoff MVP while playing on a Stanley Cup-losing team. Unscramble the names of these other winners by placing each letter in the correct order in the boxes. To help, each name starts with the bolded letter. Next, unscramble the letters in the diamond-shaped boxes to spell out the first name of our secret MVP; then the circled boxes for his family name; and the square-shaped boxes for his team.

(*Solutions are on page 118*)

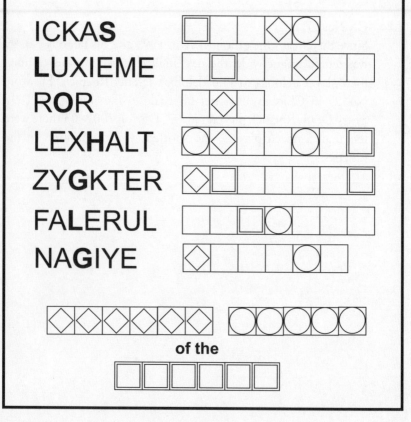

ICKA**S**

LU**X**IEME

R**O**R

LE**XH**ALT

ZY**G**KTER

FA**L**ERUL

NA**G**IYE

of the

2

"WE JUST GOT FORSBERGED."

After a 4–2 loss to Colorado during which Peter Forsberg scored three times, Calgary coach Darryl Sutter summed up the game succinctly: the Flames "just got Forsberged." All opposition teams get whacked by the Avalanche star sooner or later. As Sutter explained, "He's an old-time player. You can almost throw his stats out the window because he does so many important things that don't show up on the game sheet." In this chapter you'll need the kind of second and third effort delivered by Forsberg to score any trivia points.

(Answers are on page 23)

2.1 What is the fewest number of shots on goal recorded by an NHL scoring champion (in a minimum of 70 games)?
A. 166 shots
B. 186 shots
C. 206 shots
D. 226 shots

2.2 How many seconds did it take Boston's Mike Knuble to set the NHL record for the two fastest goals from the start of a game? It happened in 2002–03.
A. Seven seconds
B. 17 seconds
C. 27 seconds
D. 37 seconds

2.3 What is the shortest time one player has scored two goals against his former team after being traded?

A. One day

B. One week

C. Two weeks

D. One month

2.4 Who is the only defenseman to score more goals than all members of his team in one season?

A. Bobby Orr of the Boston Bruins

B. Doug Wilson of the Chicago Blackhawks

C. Carl Vadnais of the Oakland Seals

D. Kevin Hatcher of the Washington Capitals

2.5 What is highest plus-minus recorded by a player in one game?

A. Plus-6

B. Plus-8

C. Plus-10

D. Plus-12

2.6 What is the most number of game-winning goals scored by a player in one season?

A. 12 game winners

B. 16 game winners

C. 20 game winners

D. 24 game winners

2.7 What is the longest consecutive point-scoring streak by a defenseman?

A. 16 games

B. 20 games

C. 24 games

D. 28 games

2.8 Who is the first rookie defenseman to score at least 75 points in one season?
A. Ray Bourque in 1979–80
B. Larry Murphy in 1980–81
C. Gary Suter in 1985–86
D. Brian Leetch in 1988–89

2.9 Who is the first player to score 100 goals against every other team in the league?
A. Maurice Richard
B. Gordie Howe
C. Bobby Hull
D. Jean Béliveau

2.10 Who is the youngest player to score a hat trick?
A. Jaromir Jagr
B. Mario Lemieux
C. Wayne Gretzky
D. Marcel Dionne

2.11 Which player didn't score his first hat trick until he had more than 300 goals? It happened in 2002–03.
A. Adam Graves
B. Scott Mellanby
C. Trevor Linden
D. Phil Housley

2.12 After Bobby Hull, which NHLer scored the most points in his final season before joining the rival WHA during the 1970s?
A. Gordie Howe
B. John McKenzie
C. Frank Mahovlich
D. Wayne Connelly

2.13 Who was the last NHLer to score at a goal-a-game pace before Wayne Gretzky did it in 1981–82 with 92 goals in 80 games?

A. Maurice Richard
B. Gordie Howe
C. Mike Bossy
D. No one did it before Wayne Gretzky

2.14 Who is the first defenseman to record 500 career points?

A. Pierre Pilote
B. Bill Gadsby
C. Doug Harvey
D. Red Kelly

2.15 Which NHLer tied Gordie Howe's career record for 50-point seasons in 2002–03?

A. Ron Francis
B. Brett Hull
C. Chris Chelios
D. Mark Messier

2.16 Which of the following feats did Bobby and Brett Hull both accomplish?

A. A 50-goal season
B. A 500-goal career
C. A 1,000-point career
D. All of the above

2.17 If the most points for a Hart Trophy winner is Wayne Gretzky's 215 points in 1985–86, what is the lowest point total by a modern-day MVP (excluding goalies)?

A. 22 points
B. 52 points
C. 82 points
D. 112 points

2.18 Who was the first rookie in NHL history to score two penalty-shot goals in one season? It happened in 2000–01.
   A. Brad Richards of the Tampa Bay Lightning
   B. David Vyborny of the Columbus Blue Jackets
   C. Marian Gaborik of the Minnesota Wild
   D. Martin Havlat of the Ottawa Senators

2.19 When was the last time a rookie scored five goals in one game?
   A. 1936–37
   B. 1956–57
   C. 1976–77
   D. 1996–97

2.20 As of 2002–03, who was the last left-winger to win the NHL scoring race?
   A. Jaromir Jagr in 2000–01
   B. Bryan Trottier in 1978–79
   C. Guy Lafleur in 1975–76
   D. Bobby Hull in 1965–66

2.21 Which teammates hold the record for the most power-play goals in one season?
   A. Pittsburgh's Mario Lemieux and Rob Brown
   B. Philadelphia's Tim Kerr and Brian Propp
   C. Calgary's Joe Nieuwendyk and Joe Mullen
   D. Vancouver's Todd Bertuzzi and Markus Naslund

2.22 In what year did a rookie defenseman first record 50 assists in one season?
   A. 1957–58
   B. 1967–68
   C. 1977–78
   D. 1987–88

2.23 Who was the first NHLer to score 50 assists in 10 consecutive seasons?
A. Gordie Howe
B. Adam Oates
C. Wayne Gretzky
D. Bernie Federko

2.24 Which old-time great is the only player to twice lead the NHL in scoring with a team that failed to make the playoffs?
A. Bill Cowley of the Boston Bruins
B. Toe Blake of the Montreal Canadiens
C. Max Bentley of the Chicago Blackhawks
D. Sweeney Schriner of the New York Americans

2.25 Besides Gordie Howe, who is the only other 42-year-old in NHL history to get as many points as his age?
A. Alex Delvecchio
B. Igor Larionov
C. Mark Messier
D. Johnny Bucyk

2.26 What is the most games a scoring champion has missed in a season?
A. 12 games
B. 18 games
C. 24 games
D. 30 games

2.27 Who is the only goal-scoring leader not elected to an All-Star team on two occasions?
A. Blaine Stoughton
B. Peter Bondra
C. Keith Tkachuk
D. Teemu Selanne

2.28 Who scored a league-high seven points in one game in 2002–03?
A. Markus Naslund of the Vancouver Canucks
B. Peter Forsberg of the Colorado Avalanche
C. Jaromir Jagr of the Washington Capitals
D. Dany Heatley of the Atlanta Thrashers

2.29 How many fewer points did Eric Lindros score in his 81-game season of 2002–03 than in 1995–96, when he played in a previous career-high 73 games?
A. 32 points
B. 42 points
C. 52 points
D. 62 points

2.30 Bobby Orr led all NHL defensemen in scoring seven times. What was his largest single-season lead over the runner-up in points?
A. 29 points
B. 42 points
C. 60 points
D. 76 points

2.31 What is the best regular-season finish in the scoring race by a player traded mid-season?
A. Second overall
B. Fourth overall
C. Sixth overall
D. Eighth overall

2.32 Who was the first NHLer to record 100 assists in a career?
A. Frank Nighbor
B. Cy Denneny
C. Frank Boucher
D. Howie Morenz

2.33 Considering the NHL record for the fastest goal by a rookie is 15 seconds, what is the freshman record for the fastest assist?
A. 12 seconds
B. The same time, 15 seconds
C. 30 seconds
D. One minute

2.34 Which Minnesota player passed Wild coach Jacques Lemaire on the NHL all-time scoring list in 2002–03?
A. Cliff Ronning
B. Andrew Brunette
C. Marian Gaborik
D. Jim Dowd

2.35 What is the greatest number of goals scored in two consecutive games by a modern-day player?
A. Six goals
B. Seven goals
C. Eight goals
D. Nine goals

2.36 Who was the first NHLer to score 10 shorthand goals in one season?
A. Marcel Dionne of the Detroit Red Wings
B. Wayne Gretzky of the Edmonton Oilers
C. Mario Lemieux of the Pittsburgh Penguins
D. Dirk Graham of the Chicago Blackhawks

"WE JUST GOT FORSBERGED."

Answers

2.1 **A. 166 shots**

Since shot counts became available in 1967–68, only one player had won the scoring race with a shot total below 200: Bryan Trottier. Few expected anyone to break Trottier's record low of 187 shots in 1978–79, especially considering scoring leaders average about 322 shots to win the title. But in 2002–03 Peter Forsberg led the loop with 106 points and set a new mark, potting 29 goals on 166 shots, almost half the average shot-count by scoring champions. Forsberg's low total may be because he doesn't shoot enough, the only knock against hockey's best all-round player. Or it may be, as Calgary coach Darryl Sutter says, Forsberg is "an old-time player." Only twice in more than a half-century of hockey has a scoring leader had fewer goals than Forsberg. Ted Lindsay won the crown with 23 goals in 1949–50 and Stan Mikita had 28 goals in 1964–65.

2.2 **C. 27 seconds**

Knuble potted the fastest two goals from the start of a game in league history against Florida on February 14, 2003. Scoring at 0:10 and 0:27 against the Panthers' Roberto Luongo, Knuble eclipsed a 28-year-old record of 33 seconds held by Chicago's John Marks. Setting an NHL standard was Knuble's way of celebrating his 400th career game, which he recorded a week earlier against Pittsburgh.

2.3 **A. One day**

There is no record holder in this category, but Steve Thomas is probably the best candidate. Only one day after Thomas was traded by Chicago to Anaheim, he scored two goals—including the game-winner—in his first two shots against his former team. "It was weird. There were times out there when I thought I was in a red jersey," said the ex-Hawk. Thomas had scored just four goals in 69 games with the Blackhawks before his trade on March 11, 2003.

2.4   C.   Carl Vadnais of the Oakland Seals
Similar to the fate of many snipers who played in the long shadow of Wayne Gretzky, Vadnais came into the NHL at the same time as Bobby Orr. While Orr was producing the greatest regular season by a defenseman with league records for assists and points, a Stanley Cup-winning goal and four major individual trophies, Carl Vadnais was having a pretty good year with the anemic Seals in Oakland. True, it was nothing compared to what Orr had accomplished with the high-powered Bruins, but Vadnais, one of hockey's most gifted offensive defensemen of his era, led Oakland with 24 goals, the first and only time a blueliner topped his teammates in goals in regular-season play. Seals centre Earl Ingarfield recorded 21 goals that year. The only other D-man to challenge Vadnais in this category is Washington's Kevin Hatcher who shared the team lead with teammate Kelly Miller, each scoring 24 goals in 1990–91.

2.5   C.   Plus-10
Tom Bladon's lengthy but unspectacular 696-game NHL career would not raise an eyebrow today were it not for one night against the Cleveland Barons on December 11, 1977. His four goals and four assists bumped Bladon ahead of Bobby Orr's single-game seven-point defenseman record and earned the Philadelphia rearguard a whopping plus-10, a statistic unmatched today. The Flyers beat the Barons 11–1.

2.6   B.   16 game winners
Only two players in league annals have been credited with 15 or more game-winning goals in one season. Phil Esposito scored 16 game winners in back-to-back seasons of 1970–71 and 1971–72. Then, in 1983–84, Quebec's Michel Goulet earned an amazing 38 per cent of the Nordiques' 42 wins with 16 game winners.

2.7   **D. 28 games**
When it comes to scoring streaks Paul Coffey is far ahead of the pack, an illustrious group that includes Ray Bourque, Brian Leetch and Bobby Orr. None have cracked 20 games, never mind the 25-game barrier. Coffey netted 55 points in a record 28 straight games with Edmonton during 1985–86.

2.8   **B. Larry Murphy in 1980–81**
Few first-year defensemen have been afforded the ice time Murphy received in his rookie start. Coach Bob Berry believed that Murphy could easily make the transition from junior hockey to the NHL. In fact, Murphy's rookie-record 76 points was fourth in team scoring, only behind the Triple Crown Line of Marcel Dionne, Dave Taylor and Charlie Simmer, each of whom finished in the NHL's Top 10.

2.9   **B. Gordie Howe**
Yes, there were only six teams during Howe's prime, but even so this is quite a feat. Maurice Richard, for example, never popped 100 goals against all five opposition teams. Howe completed his historical six-pack by notching his 100th against Montreal in a 6–0 Detroit whitewash on February 7, 1965. The goal came against Gump Worsley, the same netminder that Howe victimized for his 500th NHL goal, three years earlier.

2.10   **A. Jaromir Jagr**
Selected fifth overall by Pittsburgh in 1990's Entry Draft, Jagr, 18, landed on a Penguin team poised for greatness. Before Mario and the boys copped their first Stanley Cup in 1991, Jagr scored his first career hat trick in a 6–2 win against Boston on February 2, 1991. Jagr was 13 days short of his 19th birthday. Gretzky scored his first hat trick on February 1, 1980—five days past his 19th birthday.

2.11   **B. Scott Mellanby**
Mellanby, the man who made the two-goal "rat trick" famous in Florida, only scored his first ever hat trick on March 6, 2003,

when he knocked home career goals 324, 325, 326 and 327 against Phoenix in a 6–3 win. Mellanby is one of the few players to reach the 300-goal mark without a hat trick. He was playing in his 1,209th career game.

2.12 C. Frank Mahovlich
A few big hockey names made the WHA legit, after Bobby Hull and goalie Gerry Cheevers, Mahovlich was the next most prominent NHL casualty who left to play for better money in the rival league. After a sterling 18-year NHL career, capped by some of his most productive seasons, including 80 points in 1973–74, the Big M split for the WHA Toronto Toros. Unlike Hull or Howe he never played in the NHL again.

2.13 A. Maurice Richard
Although a number of players recorded goal-a-game seasons during the NHL's formative years after 1917–18, it wasn't until 1944–45 when Richard scored 50 goals in 50 games that the league had a modern-day benchmark for goal scoring. No scorer duplicated Richard's achievement of a goal-a-game pace until Gretzky, 37 years later, in 1981–82.

2.14 B. Bill Gadsby
A superb two-way defenseman, Gadsby narrowly beat Doug Harvey in the race to be the first rearguard to record 500 points. Gadsby scored the league's first 500th on November 4, 1962, just months ahead of Harvey's 500th. Red Kelly, who amassed 452 points while patrolling the blueline for Detroit, would have been the first to reach to the mark, but he was converted into a centre after his trade to Toronto in 1959–60. When Gadsby retired in 1965–66, he ranked 20th among NHL scorers.

2.15 A. Ron Francis
The longevity of Howe's career has made some of his records almost unbeatable. It's unlikely Ron Francis will duplicate Howe

and score an NHL goal at 52 years old, but he tied the old man in 50-point seasons with his record 22nd in 2002–03. Francis hadn't missed a 50-point year since joining the league in 1981–82. His 22nd 50th point came on March 13, 2003, in a 5–3 Carolina loss to Philadelphia.

2.16 D. All of the above
Not only are the Hulls the only father and son duo in NHL history to achieve at least one of hockey's four most important scoring milestones—the 50-goal season, the 100-point season, the 500-goal career and the 1,000-point career—the Golden Jet and the Golden Brett have each accomplished all four benchmarks during their remarkable careers.

2.17 B. 52 points
The all-time mark for fewest regular-season points by an MVP is held by Herb Gardiner, a veteran defenseman of the disbanded western pro leagues who won the Hart as an NHL rookie at the age of 35 in 1926–27. He scored just 12 points, but between 1925–26 and 1926–27, the year Gardiner arrived, Montreal dropped from 108 to 67 goals against and rose from last place to second best overall in just one season. Based on that single-season turnaround, Gardiner didn't need big points for his MVP award. The modern-day record of 52 points is held by Toronto's Ted Kennedy, who, unlike Gardiner, won it in his last full NHL season, 1954–55. Less deserving than perhaps other players that year (Kennedy didn't finish in the top-10 scorers), the gritty Toronto captain may have won based on his years of service as one of the club's greatest stars during a run of five Cups in seven seasons. Kennedy is the last Leaf to win the Hart.

2.18 B. David Vyborny of the Columbus Blue Jackets
A few players have managed two penalty-shot goals in one season and Pavel Bure established the record at three in 1997–98, but

until Vyborny came along no rookie had ever scored more than one goal mano-a-mano. The Blue Jackets freshman scored against Chicago's Robbie Tallas on October 15, 2000, and against Nashville's Tomas Vokoun on March 19, 2001.

2.19 C. 1976–77
It was a night few will forget and a record not since duplicated by a rookie. In just his fourth NHL game, New York Ranger rookie Don Murdoch scored five times against Minnesota on October 12, 1976. He immediately became the darling of the hockey world. Murdoch picks up the story of his fifth goal with just 10 seconds on the clock in Chris McDonell's *The Game I'll Never Forget:* "I jumped out onto the ice like a kid in the candy store and glided down to the Minnesota end of the ice. That's where Espo (Phil Esposito) pulled me aside. "Listen kid," said Espo, "Stay here. Don't move from here. If I win the draw, you'll get it. If I lose the draw, don't move. I'll get it to you." I just looked at him and nodded." Murdoch stood in the exact spot where he was told to and waited. A moment later he rippled the net for his fifth of the night. Murdoch is the only teenager in NHL history to record a five-goal game.

2.20 D. Bobby Hull in 1965–66
The best chance in recent years for a left-winger to finally win the Art Ross Trophy as the NHL scoring leader came in 2002–03 when Vancouver's Markus Naslund recorded 104 points, just two points fewer than scoring leader Peter Forsberg of Colorado. But in their final game of the season, with only a tie needed to sew up the Northwest Division (which they had led since late November 2002), the Canucks "choked," in Naslund's own words, and lost 2–0 to vacation-bound Los Angeles, a team that used eight minor-leaguers. Vancouver squandered a double opportunity. They failed to clinch their first division championship in a decade and their captain missed becoming the first left-winger to capture top scoring

honours in 36 years. Bobby Hull won the award with 97 points in 1965–66. Why so long a wait for left-wingers? The hockey know-it-alls have several theories. Since most centres are left-handed, a forehand pass is a more natural and accurate pass to a right-winger than a backhand pass to a left-winger. Or another theory says that right-handed shooters fair better because they tend to fire at the goalie's stick side, often considered the weaker side compared to his glove side. Left-handed shooters are inclined to blast away across the net at the glove side. In that 36-year span, centres, led by Wayne Gretzky, Mario Lemieux and Phil Esposito, amassed 26 titles; right-wingers, including Jaromir Jagr and Guy Lafleur, captured nine titles; and defenseman Bobby Orr won two.

2.21 A. Pittsburgh's Mario Lemieux and Rob Brown
In 1988–89 the Penguins' power play usually meant one thing: a goal. It didn't matter who the opposition was or what combination of players were thrown together as a special team, Mario and the boys found a way to make their opponents pay for their transgression. Pittsburgh established an NHL record with 119 goals on the man-advantage as Lemieux (31) and Brown (24) lead the charge for a combined 55 power-play markers, the most ever by teammates in one season.

2.22 C. 1977–78
The New York Islanders' Stefan Persson was a solid-yet-unspectacular defenseman who happened to find a place on a team of great destiny. In Sweden he had very low point totals, but with the Islanders he racked up an unprecedented 50 assists in his first season. Only rookies Chris Chelios and Larry Murphy have topped Persson in this category.

2.23 D. Bernie Federko
One of the few scoring stars on the blue-collar teams of the Harry Ornest-owned Blues, Federko got a lot of ice time, playing much

of a season on two lines. He recorded this NHL first, scoring 50 assists or more between 1978–79 to 1987–88.

2.24 D. Sweeney Schriner of the New York Americans
Six players from non-playoff teams have topped the NHL in scoring, but Schriner is the only man to do it twice. The Hall of Fame forward paced the NHL in points with the lowly New York Americans during 1935–36 and 1936–37. Schriner's scoring touch caught the eye of Toronto Maple Leafs general manager Conn Smythe, who acquired the left-winger in a trade in 1939. Schriner helped the Leafs win the Cup in 1942 and 1945, but never led the loop in scoring again.

2.25 B. Igor Larionov
There is little chance of anyone ever challenging Gordie Howe as the oldest point-producing NHLer. His last season, 1979–80, was a 41-point campaign at the age of 52. But Larionov did equal another Howe mark, becoming just the second 42-year-old to record as many points as their age. In 2002–03, at 42, Larionov scored 43 points. Mark Messier was another candidate in 2002–03, but the 42-year-old legend registered 40 points. Howe had 71 points at age 42 in 1969–70.

2.26 C. 24 games
Mario Lemieux outscored Pat LaFontaine by 12 points (160 to 148) to win the scoring title in 1992–93, despite missing 24 games, a record high for a scoring champion. After sitting out seven weeks while receiving radiation treatment for Hodgkin's disease, Lemieux made a miraculous return to the Pittsburgh Penguins' lineup on March 2. Playing like a man possessed, he recorded 56 points in his last 20 games to overtake LaFontaine.

2.27 B. Peter Bondra
Since 1930–31 six goal-scoring leaders have failed to make the grade on either the first or second All-Star teams. Unlike his five

colleagues, Bondra was burned twice: in 1994–95 and 1997–98, when the right-winger was upstaged by point-scoring leader and first All-Star Jaromir Jagr twice, and second All-Stars Theo Fleury and Teemu Selanne.

2.28 **C. Jaromir Jagr of the Washington Capitals**
Jagr matched his career high with seven points on three goals and four assists as the Capitals pounded the Florida Panthers 12–2 on January 10, 2003. Although Panthers' owner Alan Cohen later complained that Washington had deliberately run up the score, Caps coach Bruce "Butch" Cassidy actually applied the brakes with his team ahead 9–0 at the end of the second period. Jagr, who played just 14 minutes in the entire game, sat out most of the third period, denying him any chance of breaking Darryl Sittler's single game record of 10 points.

2.29 **D. 62 points**
The last time Lindros played in a plus-73-game season, 1995–96, he scored 115 points with Philadelphia. The Lindros of 2002–03 shared few similarities beyond the games played stat. He scored just 53 points with the New York Rangers.

2.30 **D. 76 points**
You can get a sense of Orr's revolutionary impact on hockey by this astounding number. In 1969–70, the Bruins rearguard posted a league-high 120 points, shattering his own record for a blueliner by 56 points. The next-highest point total by a defenseman that season was 44, shared by Oakland's Carol Vadnais and Toronto's Jim McKenny. The next season, Orr turned it up another notch, amassing 139 points, which again was precisely 76 points better than runner-up J.C. Tremblay of Montreal, who had 63.

2.31 **A. Second overall**
Between 1917–18, when the NHL began operations, and 2002–03, at least 20 players dealt mid-season finished among the top

10 in league scoring. Two players, both traded from defunct NHL teams, finished second in the scoring race after their trades. Babe Dye went from Hamilton to Toronto in 1920–21 and Syd Howe moved from St. Louis to Detroit in 1934–35. In another oddity, Hall of Fame centre Duke Keats was traded in consecutive years, 1926 and 1927, and had top 10 finishes both seasons. The best placement involving a traded player since 1967–68 is John Cullen, who finished fifth overall after being dealt by Pittsburgh to Hartford in March 1991. Although Cullen amassed 110 points that year, the Penguins got Ron Francis and Ulf Samuelsson, two core players of their Stanley Cup wins in 1991 and 1992.

2.32 C. Frank Boucher
Considered the best playmaker of his day, Boucher topped the league in assists three times while centring brother wingers Bill and Bun Cook on the New York Rangers in the 1930s. The trio became the NHL's most productive unit and helped the Rangers to two Stanley Cups. Boucher earned the league's first 100th career assist in 1930–31, his fifth season. The great Howie Morenz notched his 100th the following year in 1931–32.

2.33 A. 12 seconds
The NHL Guide and Record Book lists Toronto's Gus Bodnar as the fastest goal scorer from the start of a career. His first goal came 15 seconds into a game against the New York Rangers on October 30, 1943. But who nailed the fastest point on an assist in his NHL debut and how long did he take? Fresh out of high school hockey in Massachusetts, 18-year-old Bobby Carpenter of the Washington Capitals assisted on a goal 12 seconds after the opening face-off against Buffalo on October 7, 1981. Ryan Walter scored the goal against the Sabres.

2.34 A. Cliff Ronning
On March 9, 2003, Ronning passed coach Jacques Lemaire with his 835th and 836th point to move in 98th spot on the all-time

scoring list. In an exchange in front of the press, Lemaire pointed out that Ronning needed 17 seasons to register 835 points while he did it 12 years. "Yeah, but you played with Guy Lafleur," Ronning argued. "Hey, you're playing with (Antti) Laaksonen and (Wes) Walz," Lemaire replied.

2.35 D. Nine goals
The highest goal-count in two consecutive games by one player was recorded on December 27 and 30, 1981, by Wayne Gretzky. The Great One scored four goals on December 27 and then registered his first five-goal game on December 30. It was Gretzky's 38th and 39th game of 1981–82 and capped hockey's fastest 50-goal streak. No NHLer has ever scored consecutive five-goal games. Only a few players in NHL history have scored more than five goals in one match, and none have followed up (or preceded) it with another multiple-goal effort for a two-game total better than nine goals. A few players have scored eight goals in two games; old-timers News Lalonde and Joe Malone did during the 1920s.

2.36 A. Marcel Dionne of the Detroit Red Wings
The shorthand goal is one of those wonderful glitches in the game: it really isn't supposed to happen. In Dionne's fourth and final year with Detroit, 1974–75, he scored 47 goals, more than 50 per cent of them (25 goals) on special teams, including 10 shorthanded.

Game 2

DEFUNCT TEAMS

The NHL has had its share of failed franchises. Long before Minnesota, Quebec, Hartford and Winnipeg lost their big league teams during the 1990s, many other host cities have seen their clubs tank. In this game, match these one-time or current NHL cities with the defunct team's name.

(*Solutions are on page 118*)

Part 1

1. _____	Colorado	A.	Barons
2. _____	Philadelphia	B.	Rockies
3. _____	Montreal	C.	Quakers
4. _____	Kansas City	D.	Flames
5. _____	Cleveland	E.	Scouts
6. _____	Hamilton	F.	Tigers
7. _____	Atlanta	G.	Maroons

Part 2

1. _____	Brooklyn	A.	Eagles
2. _____	California	B.	North Stars
3. _____	Ottawa	C.	Pirates
4. _____	St. Louis	D.	Senators
5. _____	Pittsburgh	E.	Nordiques
6. _____	Minnesota	F.	Golden Seals
7. _____	Quebec	G.	Americans

3
TEAM LOYALTIES

Which original coach of an expansion team has recorded the most games behind the bench? No one to date has seriously challenged Lester Patrick's reign of 604 games with the New York Rangers from 1926–27 to 1938–39, but, on March 1, 2003, Nashville coach Barry Trotz became the modern-day leader among new NHL franchises. The Predators' 5–4 win against Chicago was Trotz's 392nd game, topping Terry Crisp's 391-game run in Tampa Bay. In this chapter, we coach you on the finer points of winning, regardless of team loyalties.

(Answers are on page 41)

3.1 What is the longest stretch of one-goal victories by a team?
   A. Six wins
   B. 10 wins
   C. 16 wins
   D. 22 wins

3.2 Prior to Atlanta's Dany Heatley and Ilya Kovalchuk 1–2 finish in Calder Trophy voting in 2001–02, when was the last time a club iced teammates voted first and second as rookie of the year?
   A. 1955–56
   B. 1965–66
   C. 1975–76
   D. 1985–86

3.3 Which coach in 2001–02 tied the Islanders Al Arbour's record of improving his team's point total in five consecutive seasons?
A. Colorado's Bob Hartley
B. Carolina's Paul Maurice
C. San Jose's Darryl Sutter
D. Detroit's Scotty Bowman

3.4 Which NHL team is associated with the "334 Club"?
A. The New Jersey Devils
B. The New York Islanders
C. The New York Rangers
D. All of the above

3.5 Which NHL team used seven different goalies in 2002–03?
A. The Atlanta Thrashers
B. The Phoenix Coyotes
C. The St. Louis Blues
D. The Pittsburgh Penguins

3.6 How many current or former NHL captains did the Toronto Maple Leafs dress in 2002–03?
A. Three captains
B. Five captains
C. Seven captains
D. Nine captains

3.7 Which Montreal defenseman did Canadiens fans nickname "Breeze-by" in 2002–03?
A. Karl Dykhuis
B. Patrice Brisebois
C. Stephane Quintal
D. Patrick Traverse

3.8 Which NHL team iced the AMP line in 2002–03?

A. The Toronto Maple Leafs

B. The Detroit Red Wings

C. The Tampa Bay Lightning

D. The Colorado Avalanche

3.9 Which NHL coach was fired twice from two different teams in the final days of a winning regular-season?

A. Larry Robinson

B. Pat Burns

C. Robbie Ftorek

D. Jacques Demers

3.10 Which scoring line of the 1940s had all its members traded away at the same time?

A. Chicago's Pony Line

B. Toronto's Flying Forts Line

C. Montreal's Punch Line

D. Toronto's Kid Line

3.11 Which scoring line was the first unit with all three members inducted into the Hall of Fame?

A. Detroit's Production Line

B. Montreal's Punch Line

C. Toronto's Kid Line

D. New York Islanders' Long Island Lighting Company

3.12 What is the highest number of coaches fired during one regular season?

A. Three coaches

B. Six coaches

C. Nine coaches

D. 12 coaches

3.13 In what season did Scotty Bowman become the winningest coach in NHL history?
   A. 1979–80
   B. 1984–85
   C. 1989–90
   D. 1994–95

3.14 Who was the last former Brooklyn American to play in the NHL?
   A. Tom Anderson
   B. Kenny Mosdell
   C. Mel "Sudden Death" Hill
   D. Harry Watson

3.15 Who was the last former Cleveland Baron to play in the NHL?
   A. Gilles Meloche
   B. Walt McKechnie
   C. Randy Holt
   D. Dennis Maruk

3.16 Who was the last former Atlanta Flame to play in the NHL?
   A. Guy Chouinard
   B. Kent Nilsson
   C. Reggie Lemelin
   D. Brad Marsh

3.17 Who was the last former Kansas City Scout to play in the NHL?
   A. Wilf Paiement
   B. Guy Charron
   C. Denis Herron
   D. Gary Bergman

3.18 Who was the last former Colorado Rockie to play in the NHL?
A. Chico Resch
B. Joel Quenneville
C. Rob Ramage
D. Steve Tambellini

3.19 Which city has had the most different NHL franchises?
A. Detroit
B. Montreal
C. New York
D. Toronto

3.20 Which old-time NHL general manager threatened to replace his entire roster with players from his farm team if they didn't play better?
A. New York's Lester Patrick
B. Detroit's Jack Adams
C. Boston's Art Ross
D. Toronto's Conn Smythe

3.21 In 1992–93, the Pittsburgh Penguins set the NHL record for consecutive wins. How many games in a row did Pittsburgh win?
A. 14 games
B. 17 games
C. 20 games
D. 23 games

3.22 As of 2002–03 how many Devils teammates has New Jersey veteran Ken Daneyko played with?
A. 120 teammates
B. 170 teammates
C. 220 teammates
D. 270 teammates

3.23 Who was the first coach to win the Jack Adams Trophy as coach of the year with different teams?

A. Scotty Bowman
B. Pat Quinn
C. Pat Burns
D. Mike Keenan

3.24 Which Original Six team was the only NHL club not in favour of adopting Rule 26c, the 1956 rule change that allowed a penalized player back on the ice after the opposition scored a goal.

A. The Montreal Canadiens
B. The Chicago Blackhawks
C. The Toronto Maple Leafs
D. The New York Rangers

3.25 Teddy Saunders was featured on the cover of the Ottawa Senators team media guide in 1999–2000? Who is Teddy Saunders?

A. The first owner of the Ottawa Senators
B. The last Ottawa-born goalie to win a Stanley Cup
C. The first Ottawa Senator to score a goal
D. The last surviving member of the original Ottawa Senators

3.26 Which 1980s coach displayed the Stanley Cup in his team's dressing room to motivate players during the finals?

A. Glen Sather of the Edmonton Oilers
B. Al Arbour of the New York Islanders
C. Terry Crisp of the Calgary Flames
D. Mike Keenan of the Philadelphia Flyers

3.27 Who holds the record for winning the Jack Adams Trophy with the most different teams?

A. Jacques Demers

B. Pat Burns

C. Mike Keenan

D. Roger Neilson

TEAM LOYALTIES
Answers

3.1 **B. 10 wins**

The Anaheim Mighty Ducks broke one of hockey's longest-standing records on February 12, 2003, when they defeated Calgary in a 4–3 win, their 10th straight one-goal victory. The streak began on January 12, a 2–1 win against St. Louis. In the 14-game stretch the Ducks lost four times (twice by one-goal margins of 2–1), but beat Columbus 4–3, Minnesota 1–0, Los Angeles 6–5, Ottawa 3–2, San Jose 4–3, Calgary 3–2, Phoenix 3–2, Carolina 2–1 and, finally, the Flames 4–3. The previous record of nine was held by the 1926–27 Ottawa Senators.

3.2 **C. 1975–76**

Only eight teammates have finished 1–2 in Calder voting since the trophy was first awarded in 1933. Prior to Heatley and Kovalchuk's first and second place finishes in 2001–02, the last club with the NHL's top two rookies was the New York Islanders in 1975–76 when Bryan Trottier won the Calder as best freshman and Chico Resch finished runner-up.

3.3 **C. San Jose's Darryl Sutter**

The 2002–03 season was supposed to be the year of the Shark. Sutter had many believing his team was ready to dominate the Western Conference and rival such power clubs as Colorado, Detroit and Dallas. Sutter had tied Al Arbour's record of five straight seasons of point improvement with a five-year climb from 1997–98 to 2001–02. He also led San Jose to a franchise-record five consecutive playoff berths and one near upset against the Avalanche in the second round of the 2002 playoffs. But the bubble burst early in 2002–03. A few key players—Evgeni Nabokov and Brad Stuart—played holdout at training camp and San Jose never found its groove. The Sharks first dumped Sutter after an 8–12–2–2 start and then jettisoned Owen Nolan, Matt Bradley and Bryan Marchment in a fire sale at the trade deadline. A week later, GM Dean Lombardi was fired. San Jose finished 25th overall with a disappointing 28–37–9–8 record.

3.4   A.   The New Jersey Devils
On January 22, 1987, a good-old fashioned New Jersey blizzard dropped 15 inches of snow and created the "334 Club" as a mere 334 fans braved the road conditions to the Meadowlands to watch the 7–5 win against the Calgary Flames. Only 13 Devils made it for the start of the game, which was delayed one hour and 46 minutes.

3.5   C.   The St. Louis Blues
St. Louis had a code-blue goaltending crisis in 2002–03. No fewer than seven masked men took a turn between the Missouri pipes. The list included three complete unknowns (Cory Rudkowsky, Reinhard Divis and Curtis Sanford), two young goalies (Brent Johnson and Fred Brathwaite) that the team soured on, one goalie brought out of retirement (Tom Barrasso) and one recycled veteran (Chris Osgood) airlifted in from the New York Islanders at the trade deadline.

3.6   C.   Seven captains
After the 2003 trade deadline, the Maple Leafs had seven current or former NHL captains on their roster. In addition to captain Mats Sundin, Toronto iced former captains Alex Mogilny (Buffalo, 1993–94); Doug Gilmour (Maple Leafs, 1992–1997;

Blackhawks, 1999–2000), Bryan McCabe (New York Islanders, 1996–97), Shayne Corson (Oilers, 1994–95; Blues, 1995–96), Tom Fitzgerald (Predators, 1998–2002) and Owen Nolan (Sharks, 1998–2003).

3.7 B. Patrice Brisebois
Brisebois, the last remaining link to the Canadiens' 1993 Stanley Cup, is not the first player branded by Montreal's merciless fans and its media with a catchy but unflattering nickname. The oft-criticized Brisebois earned the "Breeze-by" moniker for his spotty defensive play, not unlike another much-criticized member of the Habs, goalie Andre "Red-Light" Racicot. As Racicot later said, "They booed Stephane Richer out of town and look what they did to Patrick (Roy). It's (Montreal) a stupid place to play but life goes on." For a short time during Montreal's ill-fated 2002–03 season, Brisebois was diagnosed with an irregular heartbeat due to work-related stress.

3.8 D. The Colorado Avalanche
The AMP line of Alex Tanguay, Milan Hejduk and Peter Forsberg was arguably the best line of 2002–03. Hejduk scored 50 goals to become the first player in Colorado history to lead the league in goals. Meanwhile, Forsberg led the league in scoring with 106 points and assists with 77. Tanguay came back from a poor season in 2001–02 to collect 26 goals and 41 assists. During the final 37 games of 2002–03 the trio combined for 59 goals and 90 assists. The line's name is an anagram of the player's first names.

3.9 C. Robbie Ftorek
Ftorek has coached three NHL teams, never lasting past two seasons with any of them. He was fired in L.A. in 1988–89 after a year and half at the helm, blown out in New Jersey during his second season with only eight games left in 1999–2000 and, three seasons later, given the hook again in his second year just weeks before the playoffs when Boston unloaded him with nine games

remaining in 2002–03. Ftorek's record was 41–20–8–5 in New Jersey and 33–28–8–4 in Boston. The best story of how Ftorek alienated himself from his players may be when he purposely scratched Ken Daneyko from the lineup in St. Louis so that the career-playing Devil wouldn't record his 1,000th game a few nights later before New Jersey fans on October 27, 1999. It was a slight never forgiven in the Devils' dressing room.

3.10 B. Toronto's Flying Forts Line
Despite a Stanley Cup in 1947, Toronto GM Conn Smythe dealt five Leafs, including the talented Flying Forts of Gus Bodnar, Bud Poile and Gaye Stewart, for defending scoring champion Max Bentley of Chicago. All three members of the Flying Forts were from Fort William, Ontario.

3.11 B. Montreal's Punch Line
Only a small number of scoring units have been inducted into the Hall of Fame. In 2002, the Islanders line of Mike Bossy, Bryan Trottier and Clark Gillies earned that distinction when Gillies was finally elected to the Hall. The first trio with full Hall of Fame membership was the Punch Line of Toe Blake, Elmer Lach and Maurice Richard, who were all inducted by 1966, just six years after Richard retired in 1960 and 18 years after the line broke up in 1948. Despite its fame, the Punch Line played together less than five seasons, but in that short time revitalized the sagging Canadiens franchise with Stanley Cups in 1944 and 1946. The line's most revered contribution to hockey is the NHL's first 50-goal season by Richard.

3.12 C. Nine coaches
Trigger-happy GMs made an all-time high nine in-season coaching changes during 1981–82 and 2000–01. Those who took the bullet in 2000–01 were Craig Hartsburg (Anaheim), Pat Burns (Boston), Don Hay (Calgary), Alpo Suhonen (Chicago), Terry Murray (Florida), Alain Vigneault (Montreal), Butch Goring

(New York Islanders), Craig Ramsay (Philadelphia) and Steve Ludzik (Tampa Bay). The most new coaches league-wide at the start of a season was recorded in 1997–98 when 10 teams had new bosses behind the bench.

3.13 B. 1984–85
Bowman's NHL mark of 1,244 wins is about as safe as Glenn Hall's record stretch of 502 games between the pipes. Neither will ever be beaten. Bowman's reign began on December 26, 1984, when the Buffalo Sabres shutout Toronto 6–0 and won their coach his 693rd victory, one more than Dick Irvin, who recorded 692 wins during his distinguished career. The coach who came closest to toppling Bowman was Al Arbour. In 1990–91, while Bowman was in the fourth year of his first retirement, Arbour hit 661 wins. Still Bowman was untouchable. He had 739 victories and was just starting the second half of his career, one that would add another 504 wins and four Stanley Cups.

3.14 B. Kenny Mosdell
The disappearance of the Brooklyn Americans created the era of the six-team NHL. Mosdell began his NHL career in the Americans' last season, 1941–42, and played through to the start of 1957–58, a total of 693 regular-season games. He later played three playoff games with Montreal in 1959, the last time a former Brooklyn American played in the NHL.

3.15 D. Dennis Maruk
The Barons completed just two NHL seasons, 1976–77 and 1977–78. Although they played to the largest seating capacity in the NHL at the time, the 18,544-seat Coliseum in Richfield, Ohio, the team struggled at the gate, playing in farm country far from downtown Cleveland. The Barons merged with Minnesota in 1978–79. Maruk played six games in 1988–89, finishing his career with the North Stars. Interestingly, Maruk was also the last active Oakland/California Seal.

3.16 B. Kent Nilsson

Among modern-day defunct NHL teams Atlanta was perhaps the most competitive club among the league's failed franchises. They completed eight seasons and made the playoffs six times between 1972–73 and 1979–80. Nilsson's first NHL season was Atlanta's last year, 1979–80. He retired in 1986–87 but returned for a six-game stint in 1995, surpassing ex-Flames Brad Marsh and Reggie Lemelin, who both retired in 1992–93.

3.17 A. Wilf Paiement

With the Blues already in St. Louis, adding a second team in Missouri was a big gamble. The hope was that a few players, such as star rookie Wilf Paiement, could turn Kansas City into an NHL town. But two teams in a southern state proved to be overkill. The league rolled snake eyes on the Scouts, sending the franchise to Denver after just two seasons in 1975–76. Paiement played 946 NHL games, including 135 with the Scouts. He retired in 1987–88.

3.18 C. Rob Ramage

The Rockies lasted six NHL seasons before turning into the New Jersey Devils in 1982–83. Ramage was Colorado's first choice overall in 1979. He played 234 games with the Rockies before moving on to seven other teams, including Calgary and Montreal where he won two Stanley Cups. Ramage retired a Philadelphia Flyer in 1993–94 after a 1,044-game career.

3.19 B. Montreal

Some cities such as Toronto and Detroit have had one franchise with three different names, other cities have played host to two different franchises, such as New York and Quebec, but Montreal was the only NHL city with three different NHL clubs: the Montreal Canadiens, Montreal Wanderers and Montreal Maroons. The Canadiens are the league's longest-existing franchise with the same name; the Wanderers played just two NHL games before they folded when their arena burned down in 1917–18; and the

Maroons are remembered as Montreal's English team, winning two Stanley Cups between 1924–25 and 1937–38.

3.20 B. Detroit's Jack Adams
Loud and always proud of his Red Wings, Jack Adams was one of hockey's toughest managers. When his two-time Stanley Cup-winning team lost the first four games of 1938–39, Adams threatened to replace the whole squad with members of Detroit's farm team, the Pittsburgh Hornets. Goalie Normie Smith received the brunt of Adams's rage. According to reports, Smith went AWOL, refusing to play again after a loss against the Rangers in New York. Adams fined and suspended him indefinitely. The two-time Cup-winning goalie threatened to retire. Adams called his bluff and Smith was gone. He never played another NHL season, returning to Detroit five years later for just six games during the war years.

3.21 B. 17 games
The amazing surge of the 1992–93 Pittsburgh Penguins was sparked by the inspirational return of Mario Lemieux to the lineup after he had spent seven weeks undergoing treatment for Hodgkin's disease, a form of cancer. With Lemieux leading the charge, Pittsburgh put together a 17-game winning streak. The streak ended on the last night of the season, when Pittsburgh was held to a 6–6 tie by the New Jersey Devils. Ironically, when the Devils made a run at the Penguins' record in 2000–01, it was Pittsburgh who stopped their streak at 13 straight wins.

3.22 C. 220 teammates
Daneyko is the most unlikely fit among the top one-team players in NHL history. A defenseman who didn't score a goal in six of his 20 seasons with New Jersey, Daneyko ranks fourth all-time with 1,288 career games, only behind such prolific scorers as Detroit's Alex Delvecchio (1,549 games), Chicago's Stan Mikita (1,394) and Steve Yzerman (1,378). During his one-team career Daneyko

played with 220 Devils teammates and outlasted 10 New Jersey head coaches. He is the only Devil to play in all of the franchise's 173 playoff games until May 13, 2003, when he was a healthy scratch for Game 2 of the New Jersey-Ottawa conference finals. Coach Pat Burns suggested the veteran made costly mistakes during a 3–2 loss in Game 1, to which Daneyko replied: "Do I buy it? No."

3.23 B. Pat Quinn
Few coaches have had as much success in as many cities as Quinn. He was voted the NHL's top bench boss in 1979–80, after piloting the Flyers to a record 35-game unbeaten streak and first-place overall. Twelve years later, Quinn won the award again when he led the formerly comatose Canucks to first place in the Smythe Division in 1991–92.

3.24 A. The Montreal Canadiens
Among the many accomplishments in Jean Béliveau's illustrious career is his 44-second hat trick, a three-goal effort scored during one power play in a game on November 5, 1955. No player has netted three goals faster since Béliveau, and that might have something to do with Rule 26c, which was created as a result of Big Jean's famous hat trick and the Canadiens firepower during the 1955–56 season. Also known as the Montreal Canadiens rule, it enabled a player serving a minor penalty to return to action after an opponent scored. The new rule was carried by a 5–1 margin at the NHL Board of Governors annual meeting in 1956. Naturally, the lone club to vote against the new legislation was Montreal. Previously, penalized players had to serve their entire two-minute sentence regardless of how many goals his team gave up while he was in the box.

3.25 D. The last surviving member of the original Ottawa Senators
Saunders played only 18 games for the old Ottawa Senators franchise, far fewer than the big names that won the club numerous

Stanley Cups during its heyday. But the current Senators club featured him on their 1999–2000 media guide because he was the last player link between the current Senators and the first Senators franchise, which folded after the 1933–34 campaign. Saunders was best known for his wrist shot. He scored one goal and three assists during his 18-game stint in Ottawa. He died on May 21, 2002, at age 90.

3.26 D. Mike Keenan of the Philadelphia Flyers
Popular superstition has it that if you touch the Stanley Cup before you compete for it—even while as a child—you will never win the trophy. But there were few believers of this myth during the 1987 finals. With Philadelphia trailing Edmonton three games to one, Keenan brought the Cup into the dressing room before Game 5 to fire up his players. The Flyers won 4–3, so Keenan repeated his ploy before Game 6, which Philadelphia won again, 3–2. The Oilers finally caught wind of Keenan's plan and before Game 7 in Edmonton, Oiler GM Glen Sather instructed team trainer Sparky Kulchisky to stash the Cup in the truck of his car. Without their pre-game fix, the Flyers were defeated 3–1. Among the 22 Philadelphia players who participated in the 1987 finals, five went on to win Cups with other teams. So too did Keenan, who sipped champagne from New York's 1994 Cup victory. So much for superstitions.

3.27 B. Pat Burns
Burns's feat indicates the perils of the profession. Being judged the coach of the year in Montreal (1989), in Toronto (1993) and in Boston (1998) is impressive, but it also means he was fired three times.

Game 3

HOCKEY CROSSWORD

(Solutions are on page 119)

Across

1. Full name of 13-year D-man mostly w. Hartford, initials A B, 1988–2001

5. _____ Roenick

7. Detroit's Sergei _____

8. _____ Messier

10. LA winger Nelson _____

11. Major department store in Canada

13. D-man Lyle _____

15. NJ's D-man Scott _____

19. Forward Vincent _____

22. Longtime Hawk, 1994 Cup winner with NYR, winger Steve _____

24. Initials of American state where Devils play

26. Retired Hartford/Washington D-man, initials S K, Scot _____

28. 1980s–1990s centre mostly w. Oilers Mark _____

30. Four-game tryout w. Pens in 1998–99, initials P S, Pavel _____

32. _____ open net

33. Father

35. Last name with the letter U three times, Buffalo-Chicago centre Christian _____

36. Goalie makes a stop or _____

37. Pittsburgh-NYR center Petr _____

Down

1. Ottawa captain Daniel _____

2. Veteran winger mostly w. Buffalo, Donald _____

3. Veteran D-man w. St. Louis-Vancouver, initials M B, Murray _____

4. Montreal D-Man Craig _____

5. Jaromir _____

6. Old-time 1940s All-Star tough guy Pat _____

8. Chicago-Edmonton winger, initials E M, Ethan _____

9. Old first name, rhymes with "hip"

12. 500-goal scorer, one-time Leaf Dave _____

14. 35-game Flyer in 1990s Yanick _____

16. 2001–02 Toronto winger Garry _____

17. Ottawa-Vancouver D-man _____ Salo

18. NYR D-man Brian _____

20. Cartilage between joints in knee, starts w. M

21. 2002–03 Pittsburgh centre Martin _____

23. _____ MacInnis

25. _____ Béliveau

27. 2001–02 Florida D-man Brad _____

28. Veteran Florida D-man-tough guy Paul _____

29. Pavel _____

31. _____ Belfour

34. Old-timer scoring champ Babe _____

4
THIS SIDE OF
KEN McAULEY

When the New York Rangers called up minor pro goalie Ken McAuley in 1943–44, they expected the worst. Ranger GM Lester Patrick had already asked the NHL to allow his team to withdraw from the league during the war years because his best players were serving overseas. When the league said play on, McAuley stepped into the breach and played all 50 games of the schedule. He won just six contests. Lester Patrick was right. The Rangers were a train-wreck as McAuley gave up an all-time high 310 goals. Almost 40 years later, Hartford's Greg Millen suffered the worst embarrassment this side of Ken McAuley when he allowed 282 goals in 60 games during 1982–83.

(Answers are on page 58)

4.1 What is the record for the longest shutout sequence by a goalie from the start of a career?
A. 60 minutes
B. 80 minutes
C. 100 minutes
D. 120 minutes

4.2 Which goalie set NHL records in both the 30-win and 40-win categories in 2002–03?
A. Curtis Joseph of the Detroit Red Wings
B. Patrick Roy of the Colorado Avalanche
C. Ed Belfour of the Toronto Maple Leafs
D. Martin Brodeur of the New Jersey Devils

4.3 What did opposing netminders Zac Bierk of Phoenix and Michael Leighton of Chicago accomplish in a Coyotes-Blackhawks game on January 8, 2003?

A. An NHL shutout first
B. An NHL shots against record
C. An NHL minutes played record
D. An NHL empty net first

4.4 What is the most number of goalies one team has iced in one season?

A. Four goalies
B. Five goalies
C. Six goalies
D. Seven goalies

4.5 Who was the first goalie to record 300 wins?

A. Johnny Bower
B. Turk Broda
C. Bill Durnan
D. Glenn Hall

4.6 What year did a goalie first jump directly from college to the NHL?

A. 1949–50
B. 1969–70
C. 1989–90
D. It's never happened

4.7 Only two goalies have recorded undefeated streaks of longer than 30 games. Both played for which team?

A. The Montreal Canadiens
B. The New York Rangers
C. The Edmonton Oilers
D. The Boston Bruins

4.8 What is the NHL record for most wins in a row by a netminder?
A. 13 wins
B. 17 wins
C. 21 wins
D. 25 wins

4.9 What is the shortest career of a Vezina Trophy winner?
A. Two games
B. 52 games
C. 152 games
D. 252 games

4.10 What is the greatest number of different teams one goalie has shutout in one season?
A. Five teams
B. Seven teams
C. Nine teams
D. 11 teams

4.11 Who was the last goalie to shutout all opposing teams in one season?
A. Tony Esposito of the Chicago Blackhawks
B. Ed Giacomin of the New York Rangers
C. Charlie Hodge of the Montreal Canadiens
D. Roger Crozier of the Detroit Red Wings

4.12 Which old-time goalie was called "The Housecleaner"?
A. John Ross Roach
B. Roy Worters
C. Georges Vezina
D. Clint Benedict

4.13 Who was the first Boston Bruins goalie to face Bobby Orr in an NHL game?
A. Dave Reece
B. Gilles Gilbert
C. Jim "Seaweed" Pettie
D. Gerry Cheevers

4.14 Which goalie called himself the Susan Lucci of hockey in 2002–03, referring to the soap opera star who finally won an Emmy after 18 years of nominations?
A. Martin Brodeur
B. Ed Belfour
C. Sean Burke
D. Patrick Lalime

4.15 Which of the following milestones did Patrick Roy reach in 2002–03?
A. First goalie to play 60,000 minutes
B. First goalie to reach 1,000 games played
C. First goalie to record 13 seasons of 30 wins
D. All of the above

4.16 What is the most number of wins recorded by an expansion-team goalie?
A. 12 wins
B. 22 wins
C. 32 wins
D. 42 wins

4.17 A photo of which goalie's scarred face was once featured in *Life* magazine to illustrate the perils of tending net in the mask-less NHL?

A. Gump Worsley

B. Johnny Bower

C. Terry Sawchuk

D. Jacques Plante

4.18 Bill Durnan, a star netminder with the Montreal Canadiens in the 1940s, was famous for what?

A. His terrible temper

B. His unusual superstitions

C. His incredibly sharp eyesight

D. His ability to catch the puck with either hand

4.19 Which coach was behind the Montreal Canadiens bench when Patrick Roy posted his first NHL win?

A. Pat Burns

B. Jacques Lemaire

C. Bob Berry

D. Jean Perron

4.20 Which goalie made a league-high 50 saves in a single game in 2002–03?

A. Ed Belfour of the Toronto Maple Leafs

B. Jose Theodore of the Montreal Canadiens

C. Tomas Vokoun of the Nashville Predators

D. Jocelyn Thibault of the Chicago Blackhawks

4.21 Which goalie set a new NHL record for most minutes played in a season in 2002–03?

A. Martin Brodeur of the New Jersey Devils

B. Marc Denis of the Columbus Blue Jackets

C. Roman Turek of the Calgary Flames

D. Roberto Luongo of the Florida Panthers

4.22 Which goalie in 2002–03 recorded the lowest goals-against average in modern-day hockey?

   A. Martin Brodeur of the New Jersey Devils

   B. Marty Turco of the Dallas Stars

   C. Patrick Roy of the Colorado Avalanche

   D. Patrick Lalime of the Ottawa Senators

4.23 Which goalie recorded the most saves in one season since 1954–55?

   A. Felix Potvin of the Toronto Maple Leafs

   B. Gump Worsley of the New York Rangers

   C. Marc Denis of the Columbus Blue Jackets

   D. Ed Johnson of the Boston Bruins

4.24 What is the highest sweater number worn by a goalie?

   A. No. 60

   B. No. 80

   C. No. 93

   D. No. 95

4.25 Since the Vezina Trophy was first awarded to the top goalie in 1927, how many winners wore their catching gloves on their right hand?

   A. There has never been a right-handed catching Vezina winner

   B. Four goalies

   C. Eight goalies

   D. 12 goalies

THIS SIDE OF KEN McAULEY

Answers

4.1 C. 100 minutes

The longest shutout sequence by a first-time goalie belongs to Detroit rookie Dave Gatherum. A fill-in for injured Terry Sawchuk, Gatherum played three games in October 1953, goosing Toronto 4–0 in his NHL debut on October 11 and then blanking Chicago until 00:21 of the third period five nights later. Gatherum earned a 2–2 tie against the Hawks and set the shutout mark at 100 minutes and 21 seconds from the start of a career. In his third game, the rookie recorded another win, but his 2–0–1 rookie record meant little when Sawchuk returned. Gatherum never played another game in the six-team NHL.

4.2 D. Martin Brodeur of the New Jersey Devils

Both Brodeur and Patrick Roy broke Tony Esposito's mark of seven consecutive 30-win seasons with their eighth straight in 2002–03, but only Brodeur reached the 40-win plateau with 41 victories. Brodeur became the first goalie in NHL history with four 40-win seasons, breaking the previous mark of three shared by old-timers Jacques Plante and Terry Sawchuk and Brodeur himself. The record for most consecutive 40-win seasons stands at two, shared by four goalies, including Brodeur who almost shattered that mark between 1997–98 and 2000–01 with win totals of 43, 39, 43 and 42. The New Jersey netminder missed establishing a new 40-win record by just one win when he netted 39 wins in 1998–99. Roy has been frustrated too. Were it not for the abbreviated 48-game schedule during 1994–95's lockout (17 wins in 43 games), Roy would have racked up 13 consecutive 30-win seasons, instead of his eight.

4.3 A. An NHL shutout first

Bierk and Leighton are the first opposing goalies to record their first career shutouts in the same game. They did it backstopping Phoenix and Chicago in the scoreless tie. Bierk stopped 40 shots and Leighton 31. The NHL has had more than 150 scoreless games since its first season in 1917–18.

4.4   D. Seven goalies
Only two teams in NHL history were forced to dress seven net-minders in one season. Quebec set the standard in 1989–90, as the Nordiques tried to stop the ugliness with Ron Tugnutt, Greg Millen, Sergei Mylnikov, Scott Gordon, Stephane Fiset, Mario Brunetta and John Tanner. Quebec ended its season last-place overall with a franchise-low of just 12 wins. The Nord's 13-year-old record was equaled in 2002–03 by the slumping St. Louis Blues, who iced Brent Johnson, Fred Brathwaite, Tom Barrasso, Cory Rudkovski, Reinhard Divis, Curtis Sandford and Chris Osgood. Injuries and ineffective rotations were the culprits for both teams, but the Blues saved some face by making the playoffs.

4.5   B. Turk Broda
Fewer than 25 netminders have hit the 300-win mark. Broda, Toronto's mainstay for 13 seasons from 1936–37 to 1951–52, reached the milestone on December 31, 1950, in a 4–2 win against Detroit.

4.6   A. 1949–50
Few NHLers came from the college ranks prior to the 1970s and even fewer made the leap without some minor pro experience. Jack Gelineau joined the Bruins late in 1948–49 after graduating from McGill University in Montreal. The next year he won the Calder Trophy as rookie of the year. Gelineau only played a couple of more seasons before quitting hockey to take a job in the insurance business.

4.7   D. The Boston Bruins
Only two goalies have managed 30 straight games without a defeat. Gerry Cheevers notched a 32-game unbeaten streak in 1971–72 with 24 wins and eight ties to earn Boston the league

title and the Stanley Cup. Almost a decade later, fellow Bruin net-minder Pete Peeters went on a tear with 26 wins and five ties in 1982–83. Peeters is the last goalie to go undefeated for 30 games

4.8 B. 17 wins

Boston Bruins goalies have carved out a few NHL marks, including the longest win streak in one season. Boston's Tiny Thompson in 1929–30 and Ross Brooks in 1973–74 set the standard at 14 straight wins. Then, two years after Ross, fellow Bruin Gilles Gilbert recorded an amazing 17-game streak between December 26, 1975, and February 29, 1976. During that two-month stretch the Bruins played 28 games split among three netminders. Gilbert saw the departure of back-up Dave Reece (who surren-dered an NHL-record 10 points to Darryl Sittler in a 11–4 wipeout to Toronto on February 7) and the arrival of Gerry Cheevers, back from oblivion and the WHA. To keep his string intact, Gilbert had some luck. In a 7–5 loss at St. Louis on January 17, he and Reece split the nets, but Reece registered the loss. In those 17 wins, Gilbert recorded one shutout and allowed just 34 goals on almost 500 shots. The Bruins scored 79 times on the opposition. The streak earned Gilbert a 33–8–10 record and the fewest losses by a starter in 1975–76.

4.9 C. 152 games

Johnny Mowers was Detroit's starter for three seasons from 1940–41 to 1942–43. During that time he played 145 games and won the Vezina Trophy and Stanley Cup before being called into military service in 1943. He played only seven more games after his return in 1946–47. Philadelphia's Pelle Lindbergh won 1985's Vezina and played in 157 games. He died in a car accident in November 1985.

4.10 D. 11 teams

In 1997–98 Dominik Hasek stormed the 26-team NHL, goosing 11 different teams in his 13-shutout season. Hasek blanked

Boston, Anaheim, Tampa Bay, Montreal, Ottawa, Washington, Pittsburgh, Calgary, Edmonton and Los Angeles once, and the New York Rangers three times.

4.11 B. Ed Giacomin of the New York Rangers

Goalies today have a snowball's chance in hell of duplicating Giacomin's shutout feat of zeroing all teams in one season. In what turned into a slow year for shutouts, just 29 in 1966–67, Giacomin ruled the league with nine, blanking Toronto three times, Chicago and Detroit twice and Montreal and Boston once in the six-team NHL. Chicago's Tony Esposito set a modern-day mark of 15 shutouts in 1969–70, recording SOs against nine of the other NHL's 11 teams. The only clubs Esposito failed to shutout were Minnesota and Giacomin's Rangers.

4.12 A. John Ross Roach

Roach earned a few nicknames during his 14-year NHL career with Toronto, New York and Detroit in the 1920s and 1930s. He stood just five-foot-five and weighed only 130 pounds. Naturally, they called him "Little Napoleon," but he was also "The House-cleaner," because he was always sweeping out his crease to keep it clear of snow. Roach's restlessness between the pipes was renowned. He wasn't a head-bobber in the Patrick Roy mould, but he had the same comportment. He was a nervous type of goalie, constantly in motion, skating back and forth between the pipes and straightening his sweater. Roach won the Stanley Cup with the Toronto St. Pats in 1922 and became the Maple Leafs first netminder in 1926–27.

4.13 C. Jim "Seaweed" Pettie

Pettie's first NHL start against the Chicago Blackhawks was doubly memorable because it came in Bobby Orr's first game against his former teammates. Orr, who had been acquired by the Hawks in a preseason trade, picked up an assist on a Dennis Hull goal in the December 1, 1976, game. Boston won 5–3.

4.14 A. Martin Brodeur

In a position known for its eccentrics, Brodeur may be the most level-headed goalie to strap on the pads. Despite nine seasons of textbook netminding, his Stanley Cups and the distinction of being the only goalie in NHL history to record 40 wins in four seasons, Brodeur could still laugh at his Vezina drought during 2002–03. "I'm the Susan Lucci of hockey. I'm like the seat filler," said Brodeur in a *Globe and Mail* story. "That's what my friends call me. I've been there three or four times, watching the other guy win..." Statistics may have been Brodeur's biggest problem in claiming the Vezina, his first only coming in 2003. New Jersey's defense is so tight, he faces far fewer shots than most goaltenders; a fact that may work against him when the general managers of the 30 clubs cast their Vezina votes.

4.15 D. All of the above

Roy has established so many important records that we would not be understating the case to say his dominance in the goaltending section of the NHL record book is Gretzky-like. And like the Great One, few of Roy's records will soon be beaten. As of 2002–03 Roy had appeared in more games than any other netminder, breaking Sawchuk's 971-game total before reaching the 1,000-game mark on January 20, 2003. Two months later in a 3–1 win against San Jose on March 31st, the Colorado goaltender eclipsed 60,000 minutes played. And in 2002–03 he earned his 30th win for a record 13th time. Along with his mark for most regular-season wins, Roy also owns some prime real estate in the playoff record book. He is the leader in victories, games played and shutouts. Amen, St. Patrick.

4.16 B. 22 wins

In their expansion year, the 2000–01 Columbus Blue Jackets won 28 games, 22 off the pads of goalie Ron Tugnutt, who tied a 74-year-old NHL record set by Lorne Chabot in the New York Rangers' first season, 1926–27. Tugnutt's 22nd victory came after making 29 saves in a 4–3 overtime win against Chicago on April 8, 2001. It equalled one of hockey's longest-standing records.

4.17 C. Terry Sawchuk
On March 4, 1966, *Life* magazine devoted a few pages to the exploits of NHL goaltenders. The most startling aspect of the layout was a nightmarish photo of Sawchuk's face. A makeup artist had retouched and highlighted his various facial scars to make them appear fresh. The grotesque patchwork of stapled tissue represented more than 200 stitches, all accumulated before Sawchuk donned a mask in 1962. The Winnipeg-born goalie battled injuries through-out his 21-year career. His ailments included a broken arm, severed wrist tendons, a fractured instep and several ruptured discs. Surgeons were constantly removing bone chips from his battered left elbow. As a grisly reminder of his pain, Sawchuk used to keep the fragments in a jar that he displayed on his mantel.

4.18 D. His ability to catch the puck with either hand
When Bill Durnan was a youngster playing for a church team in Montreal, his coach, Steve Faulkner, taught him to hold his goalie stick in either hand to make up for the fact he didn't have good lat-eral movement. By the time he reached the NHL in 1943–44, Durnan was completely ambidextrous. He wore a catching glove on both hands and during a game he would simply switch his goal stick from one hand to the other depending on which side of the net he was playing. No matter which side the shooter approached from, he faced Durnan's glove hand. The unorthodox technique helped Dr. Strangeglove win six Vezina Trophies with the Canadiens in his seven-year NHL career. In 1948–49, he blanked opposition shooters for an amazing 309 minutes and 21 seconds, a modern-day record.

4.19 B. Jacques Lemaire
The date was February 23, 1985. The Canadiens were hosting the Winnipeg Jets. Because of a rash of injuries, Roy had been called up from the Granby Bisons of the Quebec Junior Hockey

League to back up starter Doug Soetaert. The 19-year-old didn't expect to play, but just before the start of the third period, with the score knotted 4–4, Montreal coach Jacques Lemaire decided to stir the pot. "Lemaire walked into the dressing room and said, in English, 'Roy, get in the net!' My English wasn't very good. Well, it's still not very good, but there have been a lot improvements since then," Roy recalled in an ESPN interview. "I turned around and said to Guy Carbonneau, 'Did he just mention my name here?' Carbo said, 'Yeah, you're going in.' I said, 'Whoa.' It was a big thrill for me to get in net for those 20 minutes." Roy faced only two shots in the period, but got credit for his first NHL victory as Montreal scored twice to win 6–4. Soon afterwards, Roy was sent back to Granby. Lemaire, who was replaced after the season, should have kept him around. The next fall, Roy rejoined the Habs and led them to the Stanley Cup.

4.20 A. Ed Belfour of the Toronto Maple Leafs
Belfour's value to the Leafs was never more evident than during a January 4, 2003, game against the New Jersey Devils. The stumbling Leafs won 2–1 despite being outshot 51 to 19. Belfour became the first Toronto netminder to make 50 saves in one game since Felix Potvin turned aside 51 in a 4–4 tie against Los Angeles on February 13, 1997.

4.21 B. Marc Denis of the Columbus Blue Jackets
Denis ate a lot of rubber in 2002–03. He was pelted with 2,404 shots in 77 games. But he stuck it out, playing a record 4,511 minutes, to break Martin Brodeur's NHL record of 4,433 minutes, set with New Jersey in 1995–96. Denis set the new mark in the second last game of the season, a 5–5 tie with Detroit. In the team's last game, Denis got a rare treat—a night off.

4.22 B. Marty Turco of the Dallas Stars
In his first year as the Stars' No. 1 goaltender, Turco produced a 1.72 goals-against average, the stingiest average in the modern

era. Turco topped the NHL record of 1.77 set by Chicago's Tony Esposito in 1971–72 and Toronto's Al Rollins in 1950–51. Turco also recorded the second highest save percentage, .932, since the NHL began keeping the stat in 1982–83. Dominik Hasek leads all netminders with a .937 save percentage in 1998–99.

4.23 B. Gump Worsley of the New York Rangers

While playing for the defensive challenged New York teams of the 1950s, Worsley was once asked what team gave him the most trouble. He said, without missing a beat: "the Rangers." As funny as it was at the time, the Gumper wasn't joking. Playing for the Rangers was no laughing matter, as these goalie numbers reveal. No goalie has stopped more rubber in a season than Worsely. By comparison, Felix Potvin owns the hottest season since 1967–68. It was open season for shooters almost every night in 1996–97 and Potvin got burned by a lot of pucks in the Leafs' shooting gallery. He faced 2,438 shots and allowed 224 goals in 74 games.

Most Saves by Goalie in one Season*

Player	Team	Season	Shots	Saves
Gump Worsley	NYR	1955–56	2,542	2,343
Gump Worsley	NYR	1962–63	2,534	2,317
Ed Johnston	Boston	1963–64	2,446	2,235
Jacques Plante	NYR	1963–64	2,442	2,222
Felix Potvin	Toronto	1996–97	2,438	2,214
Marc Denis	Columbus	2002–03	2,404	2,172
Curtis Joseph	St. Louis	1993–94	2,382	2,169
Gump Worsley	NYR	1956–57	2,341	2,124
Bill Ranford	Edmonton	1993–94	2,325	2,089
Gump Worsley	NYR	1954–55	2,312	2,117

*Since 1954–55. Current to 2002–03

4.24 D. No. 95

Only a few goalies have broken with tradition and donned stratosphere-level sweater numbers. Jose Theodore sports a No. 60 on his Canadiens uniform, Kevin Weekes of Carolina wears No. 80 and Daren Puppa, when he played for Tampa Bay during the 1990s, donned No. 93. But Olivier Michaud hit the all-time high when he had No. 95 on his back for Montreal during 18 minutes of NHL action against Buffalo on October 26, 2001.

4.25 C. Eight goalies

As of 2002–03, only eight netminders plying the crease with a right-hand catching glove have won the Vezina Trophy. Why do so few goalies catch with their left hand? The simple explanation may be that the dominant hand is usually the right and hockey players, goalies included, have greater control of their sticks with their right hand. Therefore, netminders tend to catch with their left hand. The first Vezina winner to catch the puck with his right hand was Chicago's Charlie Gardiner. He won the award twice in 1932 and 1934. The NHL's other right-handed Vezina winners are Davey Kerr of New York Rangers; Bill Durnan, Montreal's ambidextrous goalie; Tony Esposito of Chicago; Gilles Villemure of the New York Rangers; Tom Barrasso of Buffalo; Grant Fuhr of Edmonton; and most recently, Jose Theodore of Montreal in 2002.

Game 4

GOALIE GUNNERS

Although Billy Smith is credited with the first NHL goal by a net-minder, Michel Plasse, playing with Kansas City of the Central Hockey League, is the first pro goalie to score. Plasse potted one against Oklahoma while the net was empty for an extra attacker on February 21, 1971. His goal came eight years before Smith's famous marker in 1979. In this game match the nine goalie snipers below and their NHL scoring firsts.

(Solutions are on page 119)

Jose Theodore	Billy Smith	Ron Hextall
Tiny Thompson	Grant Fuhr	Evgeni Nabokov
Damian Rhodes	Jeff Reese	Martin Brodeur

1. _____ First goalie to score an NHL goal

2. _____ First goalie to shoot and score a goal

3. _____ First goalie to score a game-winning goal

4. _____ First goalie to score a goal and record a shutout in the same game

5. _____ First goalie to shoot and score a goal and record a shutout in the same game

6. _____ First goalie to score a power-play goal

7. _____ First goalie to receive credit for an assist

8. _____ First goalie to score 10 points in one season

9. _____ First goalie to score three points in one game

5

BLACK AND BLUE AND GREEN ALL OVER

Only a few teams in NHL history have amassed a combined 300-penalty minute total in one game. On December 8, 2001, the Calgary Flames and the Anaheim Mighty Ducks cracked 300 minutes in box time, a mark not broken since April 12, 1992, when Montreal and Buffalo pounded each other for 321 minutes. Calgary and Anaheim's fight night resulted in six game misconducts, 19 fighting majors, 309 total penalty minutes and 12 games in suspensions. Anaheim won 4–0 but goalie Jean-Sébastien Giguère lost credit for the shutout when he was handed a game misconduct. In this chapter we throw a combination of punches your way with some trivia on two hockey fronts: the penalty box and the cash box.

(*Answers are on page 73*)

5.1 How many fights was Calgary sniper Jarome Iginla involved in from 1998–99 to 2002–03?
A. Iginla had no fights to his credit
B. Five fights
C. 10 fights
D. More than 15 fights

5.2 Which retired tough guy owns the NHL record for most fighting majors by a rookie?
A. Chris Nilan
B. Bob Probert
C. Mike Peluso
D. Joe Kocur

5.3 Which hockey superstar once staged a one-game strike to protest violence in hockey?

A. Bobby Hull

B. Mario Lemieux

C. Mike Bossy

D. Wayne Gretzky

5.4 When did the average weight of NHL players first reach 200 pounds?

A. 1989–90

B. 1993–94

C. 1997–98

D. 2001–02

5.5 What is the highest penalty count collected by Mario Lemieux in one game?

A. Nine penalty minutes

B. 19 penalty minutes

C. 29 penalty minutes

D. 39 penalty minutes

5.6 How many fighting majors did Philadelphia's Dave Schultz collect when he set the single-season NHL record with 472 penalty minutes in 1974–75?

A. 26 fighting majors

B. 36 fighting majors

C. 46 fighting majors

D. 56 fighting majors

5.7 Which NHL tough guy fronts a rock band called Grinder?

A. Derian Hatcher of the Dallas Stars

B. Georges Laraque of the Edmonton Oilers

C. Darren McCarty of the Detroit Red Wings

D. Matthew Barnaby of the New York Rangers

5.8 Which goalie earned his team's first ever fighting major?

A. Ron Low of the Washington Capitals

B. Billy Smith of the New York Islanders

C. Jeff Hackett of the San Jose Sharks

D. Mike Dunham of the Nashville Predators

5.9 How many fights did Wayne Gretzky have during his 20-year NHL career?

A. Three fights

B. Six fights

C. 12 fights

D. 24 fights

5.10 How much money were Bryan McCabe, Darius Kasparaitis and Rick DiPietro fined for diving in 2002–03?

A. US$100

B. US$500

C. US$1,000

D. US$5,000

5.11 On the Canadian $5 bill there is a winter scene showing kids playing hockey on an outdoor pond. What hockey number is displayed prominently in the picture?

A. No. 1

B. No. 5

C. No. 9

D. No. 99

5.12 Which player in 2002–03 earned the highest percentage of his team's payroll?

A. Pittsburgh's Mario Lemieux

B. New York Islanders' Alexei Yashin

C. Anaheim's Paul Kayira

D. Washington's Jaromir Jagr

5.13 Which hockey card trading set was first to sell for US$100?

A. 1990–91 Upper Deck

B. 1990–91 O-Pee-Chee Premier

C. 1992–93 Parkhurst

D. 1992–93 Topps Stadium Club

5.14 What is the cost for a top-of-the-line customized backyard rink?

A. CDN$50,000

B. CDN$100,000

C. CDN$150,000

D. CDN$200,000

5.15 Which NHLer paid the most money in a controversial new provincial tax aimed at players playing in Alberta?

A. Jarome Iginla of the Calgary Flames

B. Ryan Smith of the Edmonton Oilers

C. Todd Marchant of the Edmonton Oilers

D. Craig Conroy of the Calgary Flames

5.16 Which town in Saskatchewan made national headlines in 2002 in an attempt to raise money to save its community hockey rink?

A. Kelvington, Saskatchewan

B. Wapella, Saskatchewan

C. Bellegarde, Saskatchewan

D. Saskatoon, Saskatchewan

5.17 Despite the NHL's rookie salary cap, how much did Atlanta rookies Ilya Kovalchuk and Dany Heatley make during 2001–02?

A. US$1 million

B. US$2 million

C. US$3 million

D. US$4 million

5.18 What was the admission price to Wayne Gretzky's fantasy camp in 2003?
  A. US$3,999
  B. US$6,999
  C. US$9,999
  D. US$12,999

5.19 How much money did the Canadian government spend on Maurice Richard memorabilia in a 2002 auction?
  A. CDN$75,000
  B. CDN$150,000
  C. CDN$300,000
  D. CDN$600,000

5.20 How many hockey sticks are bought each year in North America?
  A. 500,000
  B. One million
  C. Three million
  D. Five million

5.21 Which NHL club promised its season-ticket holders a refund if the team didn't make the playoffs in 2002–03?
  A. The Atlanta Thrashers
  B. The Nashville Predators
  C. The Los Angeles Kings
  D. The Calgary Flames

BLACK AND BLUE AND GREEN ALL OVER
Answers

5.1   D. More than 15 fights

Iginla's dance card has been filled with 17 fights since 1998–99, one of the highest numbers ever by a scoring leader in a five-year period. His soft-hands-hard-knuckles approach to the game draws much debate, especially every time the Flames' leading scorer gets into a scrap. "Jarome's probably one of the toughest guys in here, if not the toughest. But that's not his job. His job is to stay on the ice and help us all in other areas," said veteran scrapper Bob Boughner in a *National Post* story. Flames head coach Darryl Sutter counters with: "Hey, I'm not saying Jarome Iginla has to fight. But it sure is a helluva lot easier for Jarome Iginla when he gets three more feet out there."

5.2   D. Joe Kocur

Kocur hit the league hard in 1985–86. The Detroit Red Wings recruit dropped his gloves and slugged it out 36 times in just 59 games, which set not just a new rookie record but an NHL record as well. Until broken bones in his hands forced him to cut back on hostilities, Kocur was the NHL's most feared knockout artist. During the late 1980s, he and fellow Red Wing pugilist Bob Probert were known as the Bruise Brothers.

5.3   A. Bobby Hull

The Golden Jet once sat out a game with the WHA's Winnipeg Jets to protest the level of violence in the league. Hull was especially upset by the physical abuse that his talented Swedish linemates, Anders Hedberg and Ulf Nilsson, were receiving. Hedberg and Nilsson played through the mayhem and paved the way for the acceptance of Europeans into the professional North American ranks.

5.4   C. 1997–98

Small-framed hockey players are a dying breed. Today's pro scouts wouldn't give Hall of Fame smurfs like Henri Richard (five-foot-seven, 160 pounds) or Dave Keon (five-foot-nine, 165 pounds) a second glance. In 1981–82, the average NHLer stood six feet tall and weighed 188.1 pounds. In 1997–98 the average player weight broke 200 pounds with a mean of 200.2 pounds. By 2002–03, the average height had reached six-foot-one and the average weight had risen to 204.1 pounds.

5.5   C. 29 penalty minutes

On February 6, 2003, Mario Lemieux broke his personal career high of 24 penalty minutes when he received minor penalties for slashing and instigating, a major penalty for fighting, a 10-minute misconduct and a game misconduct, for a total of 29 penalty minutes in the 6–0 loss to Florida. Lemieux's penalties came with 5:12 remaining in the Pittsburgh defeat. Furious over a second-period cross-check from Florida defenseman Brad Ference, Lemieux slashed Ference's wrist, then dropped his gloves and began pummeling the Panther enforcer. It wasn't as pretty as a Lemieux power-play goal, but the point was made. It was Super Mario's first fighting major in regular-season play since a tangle with Washington's Bobby Gould on March 20, 1987.

5.6   A. 26 fighting majors

Considering the record for most fighting majors in a single season is 39, set by Paul Laus of the Panthers in 1996–97, Schultz's rap sheet looks almost modest. The Flyers lead goon supplemented his 130 fighting minutes with 122 minutes on 61 minors and a whopping 220 minutes on misconducts.

5.7   C. Darren McCarty of the Detroit Red Wings

McCarty, who is involved in several charity causes, is also the founder and the lead singer of a Michigan rock band called Grinder. The band, which cites the Clash and MC5 as its musical influences, recorded a CD to raise funds for the families of former Red Wing defenseman Vladimir Konstantinov and trainer Sergei Mnatsakanov, who both suffered serious injuries in a car accident in June 1997.

5.8 B. Billy Smith of the New York Islanders
It's not hard to fathom this from Battlin' Billy Smith, a guy who often refused to shake hands with winning playoff opponents. Smith once said: "I just try to give myself a little extra working room." On this occasion, October 21, 1972, Smith dropped the gloves with New York Rangers winger Rod Gilbert.

5.9 A. Three fights
By tough guy standards The Great One really didn't fight, he was more of a sweater tugger. His three bouts were against Chicago's Doug Lecuyer on March 14, 1980, Neal Broten of the Minnesota North Stars on December 22, 1982, and with Bob Murray of the Blackhawks on March 7, 1984. Gretzky's most memorable fight was against Murray. "I swung at him and he blocked it and knocked me down. He said, 'Had enough?' I said, 'Yes,' and that was the fight," Gretzky said. Gretzky also collected 577 penalty minutes during his 20-year career.

5.10 C. US$1,000
A number of players were outed for diving during the NHL's first-ever crackdown in 2002–03. McCabe, Kasparaitis and DiPietro were among a slew of players fined US$1,000 for diving or faking. Perhaps more embarrassing, their names were listed in all dressing rooms throughout the league. McCabe was most vocal after an incident with Vancouver's Todd Bertuzzi in March 2003. "They don't call half the (crap) that goes on," he told the *Toronto Star.* "I get speared in the (groin) the play before, then I get punched in the head and I go down and it's a dive?" More incensed may be Edmonton's Marty Reasoner and Calgary's Oleg Saprykin, who figured they were owed penalty shots after being hauled down on a

breakaway during separate games in mid-March. Instead, both were called for diving and took penalties for their tumble. Which begs the question: Who would ever dive on a breakaway? Mario Lemieux also weighed in on the NHL's new diving policy. "I don't think it's the place of the NHL to try to embarrass players. If they would just call the obstruction, nobody would have to dive," said Lemieux.

5.11   C. No. 9
On the back of the Canadian $5 bill is an image of kids tobogganing, learning to skate and playing hockey. Four children are playing pick-up hockey and one girl is wearing a No. 9 jersey, in memory of Montreal Canadiens legend Maurice Richard. Next to the illustration is Quebecois-writer Roch Carrier's words from his story *The Hockey Sweater:* "The winters of my childhood were long long seasons. We lived in three places—the school, the church and the skating-rink—but our real life was on the skating-rink." Keeping the kids company on the reverse side of the $5 note is one-time Canadian Prime Minister Sir Wilfred Laurier. When it was introduced in March 2002 the new $5 bill was worth only about US$3.10.

5.12   A. Pittsburgh's Mario Lemieux
Since team payrolls fluctuate slightly throughout the year because of trades, this answer depends on when you do the math. At the start of 2002–03 Paul Kayira's US$10-million salary took a whooping 25.6 per cent of Anaheim's player payout of US$39 million. After the March 2003 trade deadline, which our answer is based on, the Mighty Ducks bumped its payroll to US$46 million, while Pittsburgh dumped players and dropped their payroll to US$22.8 million, making Lemieux the highest wage earner as a percentage of total team payroll. Lemieux earned US$5.25 million or 23 per cent of the Penguins' payroll. Jagr made 22.1 per cent (US$11.5 million of $52 million), Kariya 21.7 per cent (US$10 million of $46 million) and Alexei Yashin 20 per cent (US$7.4 million of $37 million).

5.13 B. 1990–91 O-Pee-Chee Premier

In the 1960s, a pack of hockey cards with bubble gum cost a nickel. When the hockey card boom hit in 1990, cards went upscale, the bubble gum disappeared and with it went any sense of innocence. The first set to blast past the US$100 mark was 1990–91 O-Pee-Chee Premier, a relatively tiny 132-card issue, highly prized because of its low production numbers and a batch of hot-shot rookies.

5.14 C. CDN$150,000

The backyard rink is no longer a matter of hammering a few planks together and then standing around in the freezing cold with a garden hose. The 2003 version of the traditional Canadian experience can cost parents from CDN$20,000 to CDN$150,000. And a little more if you want to soup-up your garden tractor into a miniature Zamboni. The new "personal" rinks are the idea of former NHLer Dave Gagner of Custom Ice Rinks Inc. His CDN$20,000 "do-it-yourself" kit has everything to build a 20-foot-by-30-foot rink, including refrigeration pipes that can be stored each spring. For CDN$150,000 Gagner will construct a concrete pad and high efficiency glycol refrigeration system that will defy Mother Nature during warm spells. High boards, glass, goal nets, night lights and electricity are extra.

5.15 A. Jarome Iginla of the Calgary Flames

As of 2002–03 all NHLers were subject to a 12.5 per cent tax on the money they earned while playing in Alberta. The hardest hit were members of the Oilers and Flames who played half their games in the province. Iginla, the best-paid player between the two teams with a salary of US$5.5 million, doled out approximately US$165,000. The players' tax is estimated to produce about US$6 million in annual revenue, with most of the money going to team owners in Edmonton and Calgary.

5.16 C. Bellegarde, Saskatchewan

Rather than see their aging rink close because of debts of CDN$5,000, Bellegarde's 41 residents held a local contest to raise money to keep the lights on. Participants had to guess which day in spring a 1968 Chevrolet Bel Air would break through one metre of ice on a man-made pond. Tickets were sold and the town raised CDN$2,000, just enough to keep the rink open through the winter. But then the *National Post* ran a front-page story and started their own free version of the contest. Soon Molson Inc. was on board, and through their Local Heroes fund, the brewery donated CDN$10,000 to save the rink. The newspaper contest included a grand prize of a free trip to Bellegarde. The rusted old Chevy finally sank on April 14, 2002. There were 14 contestants who predicted that date. In a run-off draw Jacques Dion of Asbestos, Quebec, won the prize.

5.17 D. US$4 million

After the 1994–95 collective bargaining agreement, the NHL supposedly had controls on salaries, especially for players in the entry level system. But player agents soon found a way to circumvent the limits of the cap by establishing a player bonus structure that required the Atlanta Thrashers to pay rookie sensations Kovalchuk and Heatley, US$4.375 million and US$4.195 million respectively. Heatley and Kovalchuk were 1–2 in the rookie scoring race and in Calder Trophy votes for rookie of the year.

5.18 C. US$9,999

Following in the footsteps of football's Joe Montana and basketball's Michael Jordan, Wayne Gretzky held his first-ever fantasy camp for hockey's well-heeled fans. The US$9,999 price tag, a neat tie-in to the game's most famous number, included airfare, luxury accommodations, meals, and playing with and against Gretzky and other former pros such as Paul Coffey and Russ Courtnall. The four-day camp with a guest list for 72 participants was held in Scottsdale, Arizona.

5.19 D. CDN$600,000

In a 2002 Internet auction held by the family of the late Maurice Richard, the Canadian government spent CDN$600,000 to buy 47 items of sports memorabilia belonging to the legendary star. On the block were autographed hockey sticks, pucks, trophies, as well as a 1959 Stanley Cup ring and a 1953–54 contract (hand written on a piece of scrap paper), under which Richard was paid a salary of CDN$15,000. The highest bids were for Richard's game-worn jerseys. The price of his No. 9 sweater from the 1959 Stanley Cup championship climbed to US$60,000; and his 1949 All-Star game jersey drew US$15,000. The auction received bids from sports fans and collectors around the world. The 47 items will be housed at the Canadian Museum of Civilization in Hull, Quebec.

5.20 D. Five million

The global stick market is estimated at US$100 million annually or about five million pieces are bought each year, according to figures from Bruce Dowbiggin's *The Stick*. Among elite players, composite or graphite sticks are slowly being favoured over wood-based sticks. But because of the cost differential between the two kinds of sticks, wood or fibreglass still dominate the public market. The cost of a graphite stick is still too expensive for many consumers.

5.21 B. The Nashville Predators

After a disappointing finish in 2001–02, Predators owner Craig Leipold told fans that 2002–03's season-ticket price increase would be refunded if the team didn't make postseason. Without the offer, a club survey of season-ticket subscribers predicted only 70 per cent would renew. With the offer in place, the Predators managed to attract 83 per cent of their fans back, even though there was almost no upgrade in player personnel from the previous year. As it turned out, Nashville finished 24th overall, missed the playoffs by nine points and Leipold paid back the ticket-price increase to his customers. In a related story, an auditor determined the team is costing Nashville taxpayers about US$7 million per year.

Game 5

REARGUARD RECORDS

The NHL record books are home to the league's most famous defensemen. Listed below are the first names of 22 record-setting goal scorers, point producers, plus-minus leaders and award winners who have plied the blueline. Once you figure out their family names, find them in the puzzle by reading across, down or diagonally. Following our example of Larry ROBINSON, connect the family names using letters no more than once. Start with the letters printed in heavy type.

(*Solutions are on page 120*)

Nicklas _____   Paul _____

Ray _____   Al _____

Doug _____   Chris _____

Rob _____   Bobby _____

Phil _____   Denis _____

Larry _____   Larry _____

Gary _____   Ian _____

Brian _____   Chris _____

Steve _____   Tom _____

Serge _____   Doug _____

Rod _____   Eddie _____

L	I	W	U	M		O	E	N	S	P
S	P	R	C	L	I	R	B	H	E	R
H	O	N	H	E	R	O	S	O	C	O
Y	T	L	A	D	O	N	U	Y	U	N
R	U	B	I	U	Q	R	E	D	G	L
R	O	B	E	N	R	V	R	E	S	E
N	S	L	S	A	Y	O	M	H	O	E
I	B	Y	I	O	H	E	R	R	E	T
R	N	U	A	D	N	T	L	S	C	H
E	N	L	W	G	S	D	R	A	U	S
T	I	S	L	A	N	Y	H	O	V	A
C	U	N	L	O	P	E	F	F	O	E
A	M	I	V	T		B	L	A	K	C

81

6

"So Much For Technology, Eh?"

At the 2003 All-Star game in Florida, the hardest-shot competition was won by a player using a wooden stick. True or False? In this chapter, some simple truths about the game, including the old master-blaster himself, Al MacInnis, who won the hardest shooter event at the NHL SuperSkills for a seventh time with a 98.9 MPH screamer. One of the few NHLers to resist the new composite metal sticks, MacInnis fired his bullet with a Sher-Wood brand woodie. In characteristic Canadian style, MacInnis later said: "So much for technology, eh?"

(Answers are on page 86)

6.1 Rink netting prevents about 10 pucks per game from going into the crowd. **True or False?**

6.2 No player has ever led his team in goals, assists, points and penalty minutes in the same season. **True or False?**

6.3 Although Toronto's Darcy Tucker wasn't penalized or suspended for a cheap shot hit that blew out the knee of Islander captain Michael Peca during the 2002 playoffs, that cheap shot was included in an NHL tape of unacceptable hits circulated to every club during the 2002–03 pre-season. **True or False?**

6.4 Despite winning five Art Ross Trophies, Jaromir Jagr did not win the NHL scoring title during his most productive offensive year. **True or False?**

6.5 No NHLer has ever won a Stanley Cup in both his first and last seasons of a 10-year career. **True or False?**

6.6 NHL teams only painted their gloves the same colour as their uniforms during the 1970s. **True or False?**

6.7 No player has ever recorded 500 penalty minutes in a career during the playoffs. **True or False?**

6.8 After being marketed by his team as a potential U.S. presidential candidate during the 2000 American election, Columbus Blue Jackets goalie Ron Tugnutt actually received some votes. **True or False?**

6.9 After scoring his first goal in 256 consecutive games, New Jersey defenseman Ken Daneyko kept the puck. **True or False?**

6.10 No player has ever scored his 500th goal before turning 30 years old. **True or False?**

6.11 Ray Bourque is the oldest player to score a goal in the Stanley Cup finals. **True or False?**

6.12 The first crest on the Boston Bruins jersey Bruins was the familiar spoked B. **True or False?**

6.13 The Vancouver Canucks franchise actually made money in 2002–03. **True or False?**

6.14 No brothers have ever captained Stanley Cup champions. **True or False?**

6.15 Wayne Gretzky is the first NHLer to record more assists than anyone else had points in one season. **True or False?**

6.16 The NHL's most efficient power play since expansion in 1967 belongs to the Montreal Canadiens. **True or False?**

6.17 The Pittsburgh Penguins still held Alexei Kovalev Bobblehead Night at the Mellon Arena in March 2003 even though the Russian forward had been traded to the New York Rangers a month earlier. **True or False?**

6.18 No non-goalie has ever worn No. 1 on his sweater. **True or False?**

6.19 No goalie has recorded 100 playoff wins. **True or False?**

6.20 The lowest sweater number that has not been retired by an NHL team is 13. **True or False?**

6.21 Bobby Orr is the first defenseman to score more points than every playoff scorer in one season. **True or False?**

6.22 No NHLer since 1967–68 has won the goal-scoring race with less than 10 power-play goals. **True or False?**

6.23 The odds of becoming an NHL star are approximately 15,000 to 1. **True or False?**

6.24 Mario Lemieux is the only player to return to play full-time in the NHL after spending three years in retirement. **True or False?**

6.25 Despite capturing the 2003 Stanley Cup with three shutouts in the finals, New Jersey's Martin Brodeur was not named playoff MVP. **True or False?**

6.26 Gordie Howe scored his final regular-season goal on an assist by a player who was named after him. **True or False?**

6.27 The St. Louis Blues are the only NHL team to lose three consecutive Stanley Cup finals. **True or False?**

6.28 The first NHL team to put a hockey stick on their crest is a defunct team from St. Louis. **True or False?**

6.29 No player has ever been voted to an NHL All-Star team after his death. **True or False?**

6.30 During her 12-day Golden Jubilee visit to Canada in October 2002, Queen Elizabeth II attended an NHL exhibition game and at the ceremonial face-off dropped a perfect puck. **True or False?**

6.31 Even though the 1995 Calgary Flames set the NHL record for most goals by one team in a playoff series that went seven games, they still lost that playoff round. **True or False?**

6.32 The first goal-scoring leader with more than 30 power-play goals was Wayne Gretzky. **True or False?**

6.33 While playing together in Florida, Pavel and Valeri only combined for one goal as Panthers. It came when Valeri assisted on Pavel's 400th career goal. **True or False?**

6.34 As of 2002, the last four rookie coaches to win the Stanley Cup all coached the Montreal Canadiens to the championship. **True or False?**

6.35 Every No. 1 overall pick in the NHL draft has gone on to play in the NHL. **True or False?**

"So Much For Technology, Eh?"

Answers

6.1 **True.**

On average 10 pucks are saved every game because of protective netting above the glass behind each goal. Rink netting was first installed in all NHL arenas in 2002–03 after a teenage fan was hit in the head by a deflected shot from Columbus centre Espen Knutsen during a March 16, 2002, game between the Blue Jackets and the Calgary Flames at Nationwide Arena in Columbus. The fan, 13-year-old Brittanie Cecil, died two days later in hospital. It was the first such fatality in the NHL's 85-year history. In a related story, while most teams went with black netting in the end zones, Philadelphia was the first club to switch to a clear mesh, which was initially criticized for refracting the light and distorting the view. An average of 20 to 30 pucks are still used in each NHL match.

6.2 **False.**

This feat is not so remarkable. It was recently accomplished by Darcy Tucker with Tampa Bay in 1998–99 and Theo Fleury with Calgary in 1997–98. In 1999–2000 Boston's Joe Thornton led in all three offensive categories with a 23–37–60 record while compiling a club-high 82 minutes in the box.

6.3 **True.**

In its November 2002 issue, *Sports Illustrated* called the Toronto Maple Leafs the most-hated club in hockey. A number of players were quoted, describing the city as home to "the NHL's most notorious whiners, divers and cheap-shot artists." The feature article by senior writer Michael Farber targeted such Leafs as Tie Domi, Shayne Corson and Darcy Tucker for yapping too much, hitting too low and diving too often. Opposing players also believe the Leafs are favoured by the league, citing the example of Tucker's unpenalized "low bridge" cheap shot on Peca. "That was crap," Ottawa tough guy Rob Ray said in *SI*, "not fining or suspending him and sending out the tape saying this can't happen. Why didn't they do anything when this happened?"

6.4 True.
Jagr actually scored his highest offensive numbers in a year when he was second in the scoring race. In 1995–96 Jagr averaged 1.82 points per game, for a total of 149 points in 82 games. He finished runner-up to Pittsburgh teammate Mario Lemieux, who led the league with 161 points.

6.5 False.
To date, Boston's Cooney Weiland is the only NHLer with a decade-long career that began and ended with a championship. He won it all in 1929 as a member of the famous Dynamite Line with Dit Clapper and Dutch Gainor, then moved on to Ottawa and Detroit before returning to Beantown for another Cup run in 1939, his final season.

6.6 False.
The Rangers led the shift to colour coordination, painting their neutral-coloured gloves red, white and blue to match their uniforms in 1957–58. The last fashion holdout was the Detroit Red Wings, who waited until 1967 before making the switch.

6.7 False.
The 500-minute plateau in the playoffs has been reached by only three players: Claude Lemieux (529 minutes), Chris Nilan (541 minutes) and Dale Hunter, hockey's career playoff penalty leader at a whooping 729 minutes. Hunter became the first 500-minute man during Washington's postseason drive in 1989–90, just one year ahead of Chris Nilan, who hit 500 minutes in 1991.

6.8 True.
After the votes were counted in Columbus, the *Hockey News* reported that Tugnutt earned 12 votes for president during the

American election in November 2000. During the presidential race Tugnutt went 5–1–1 with a red-hot .945 save percentage, prompting the Blue Jackets' marketing department to sell their netminder as a candidate in Ohio. Tugnutt is Canadian.

6.9   True.

Daneyko ended his NHL record dry-spell of 256 straight games with a goal against goalie Martin Biron in a 2–1 New Jersey win at Buffalo on October 25, 2002. Daneyko, the longest serving member of the Devils, last scored a regular-season goal on February 9, 1999, against Vancouver. He broke Rich Pilon's futility mark of 245 games without a goal in April 2002. (He did score a playoff goal against Dallas during the 2000 Stanley Cup finals. Goalie Ed Belfour blamed an over-the-counter cold medicine for affecting his game.) Daneyko takes it all in stride, secure in his defensive role on the Devils and his relationship with GM Lou Lamoriello. "I'm like an NHL lineman. I score about every five years." After 256 games without a goal you can be sure Daneyko kept the puck, just to make sure he wasn't dreaming.

6.10   False.

Only Wayne Gretzky (24.11 years) and Mike Bossy (29.11 years) have notched their 500th before turning 30. Both players recorded their No. 500 into an empty net.

6.11   False.

Bourque was 40 years, 154 days when he scored a goal against New Jersey in a 3–1 Colorado win on May 31, 2001. A year later, Detroit's Igor Larionov bested Bourque to become the eldest greybeard with a final series goal against Carolina at 14:47 of the third overtime period on June 9, 2002. Larionov, at 41 years, 188 days, had just broken his own record, set hours earlier after scoring a second period goal. Detroit won 3–2.

6.12 False.

Unlike Toronto's maple leaf or Detroit's winged wheel, Boston's spoked B wasn't featured on the Bruins uniforms for a quarter of a century. The crest was originally a bear and later a simple B. The spoked B was adopted in 1948–49 to commemorate the team's 25th anniversary.

6.13 True.

After years of losing on the ice and at the box office, the Canucks finally produced a winning season and turned a small profit in 2002–03. The club finished seventh overall with 104 points and sold out 37 regular-season games. Eight home playoff games and the slide of the U.S. dollar also contributed to Vancouver's positive bottom line. According to the team's chief operating officer, Dave Cobb, a one-cent shift in the exchange rate means about CDN$300,000 per year to the Canucks.

6.14 False.

Montreal's Maurice and Henri Richard are the only siblings in NHL history to captain their teams to the Cup. Maurice four times during the 1950s and Henri twice in the early 1970s.

6.15 False.

A top playmaker in the Wayne Gretzky mould, Bill Cowley could see the whole ice. He recorded 45 assists with Boston in 1940–41, one point better than five runners-up in the NHL scoring race. The only other NHLer to match Cowley's feat was Gretzky himself, who amassed more assists than anybody else's point total on three occasions, 1982–83, 1985–86 and 1986–87.

6.16 True.

It rarely paid to take a penalty against the Scotty Bowman-led Montreal Canadiens. In 1977–78 Bowman's special teams scored 31.9 per cent of the time they iced an extra attacker. The raw numbers are even more impressive. Montreal amassed 73 power-play goals on 229 advantages, with Guy Lafleur (15) and Steve Shutt (16) accounting for 31 goals. According to Elias Sports Bureau, Montreal recorded the league's best power-play percentage since expansion in 1967. Bowman's Canadiens lost just 10 games that season.

6.17 True.

Despite the fact that Kovalev had been traded February 10 to the New York Rangers, the Penguins still gave out about 16,000 Alexei Kovalev bobblehead dolls at their March 6 match-up against Carolina. According to reports, the club did not want to disappoint their fans. Instead, how about a win to bring the fans back? The game was a sellout, but the Pens lost to the Hurricanes 4–0.

6.18 False.

The circumstances under which Montreal defenseman Herb Gardiner broke hockey's longstanding tradition and wore No. 1 during 1926–27 and 1927–28 can be traced back to November 28, 1925 and the final game of Canadiens great Georges Vezina. After appearing in 325 consecutive regular-season games, Vezina was forced to retire because of tuberculosis. Sadly, the Hall of Fame netminder died months later. Out of respect no Canadiens goalie donned No. 1 for four years until George Hainsworth in 1929–30. During that time the No. 1 sweater was handed to a couple of defensemen. First it went to Gardiner and when he was traded, D-man Marty Burke took the number. Babe Seibert, another rearguard, also wore No. 1 for Montreal in the late 1930s.

6.19 False.

Patrick Roy is the only netminder in league history to hit triple-digit numbers with 151 playoff wins. He passed the century plateau on April 24, 1999, in Colorado's 3–1 victory against San Jose. Grant Fuhr trails Roy with 92 career wins.

6.20 True.

With so few players wearing unlucky No. 13, none of the NHL's 30 franchises will retire the number anytime soon. One possible candidate who could change the league's lowest unretired number from No. 13 to No. 20 (the next lowest number not retired) may be Toronto captain Mats Sundin. But that is an unlikely scenario, considering Toronto's weird policy of differentiating between retired and honoured numbers. As great as Frank Mahovlich, Johnny Bower and Tim Horton were to the Maple Leafs, their numbers have only been honoured, not retired. Of course, the highest number not retired by a team is No. 98.

6.21 False.

Bobby Orr in 1972 and Pierre Pilote in 1961 shared the playoff scoring lead during their respective years, but the first rearguard with more points than all scorers was Calgary's Al MacInnis in 1989. MacInnis amassed his league-leading 31 points on seven goals and 24 assists. Twenty-six points came during MacInnis's 17-game consecutive point-scoring streak, which equalled the second-longest in postseason play and the longest ever by a defenseman.

6.22 False.

Conventional wisdom suggests you have to capitalize on the power play to put up big goal numbers. But there are a few exceptions. Since the NHL began compiling power-play stats in 1967–68, four players—Bobby Hull, Steve Shutt, Wayne Gretzky and Keith Tkachuk—have led the league in goals while counting fewer than 10 on the power play. Hull did it first, tallying only eight of his league-high 44 goals on the man advantage in 1967–68.

6.23 True.

In a study titled *The Straight Facts About Making It In Pro Hockey,* researcher/author Jim Parcels tracked 30,000 children who played hockey in Ontario, all of whom were born in 1975. By the age of

15, three-quarters of the children had given up the sport. At 16 years old, only 232 were drafted by the OHL, and only 105 ever played in an OHL game. At the NHL draft two years later, only 48 were selected and of those only 26 played an NHL game. Two players—Todd Bertuzzi and Jason Allison—among that original group of 30,000 are NHL stars today. There are a few ways to climb the hockey hierarchy and play at the NHL level, but the overwhelming odds don't change much in another draft year, with another junior league or with a scholarship to an American college.

6.24 False.

Although Mario Lemieux's comeback has been the most successful of any retired NHL player, he is not the only skater to return to action after retiring. Ted Lindsay rejoined the Detroit Red Wings in 1964–65, after spending four years in retirement, and New York Rangers star centre Frank Boucher spent five years off the ice, four of them coaching the Rangers, before suiting up again as a player-coach in 1944–45, when the club's roster was decimated by war enlistments. The 42-year-old Boucher tallied 14 points in 15 games with the Blueshirts before retiring for good. Toronto's Carl Brewer retired four times from hockey, in 1965, 1972, 1974 and finally in 1980. His longest stint away from the game was for five seasons during the 1970s. He returned for 20 games in 1979–80.

6.25 True.

Under most circumstances notching three shutouts in the finals should be a lock for the Conn Smythe Trophy. But before the 2003 finals began MVP voters were already picking their candidate: Jean-Sébastien Giguère. The Mighty Ducks netminder had carried Anaheim through three playoff rounds by defeating powerhouse teams Detroit and Dallas, and then eliminating the up-start Minnesota Wild. In the finals against New Jersey, Giguère pushed the Devils to the limit before losing Game 7. Conn Smythe voters (professional hockey writers) had their man, this despite Brodeur's three 3–0 wins against Anaheim to capture the Cup. No goalie had accomplished such a feat since Frank McCool stunned Detroit with a trio of shutouts in 1945.

6.26 True.
On April 6, 1980, Howe, a member of the Hartford Whalers, scored his last regular-season goal against Detroit's Rogie Vachon. Assisting on the play were Ray Allison and Detroit native Gordie Roberts, who was named after Howe when the Red Wing star was at his peak during the 1950s. Roberts broke in the NHL in 1979–80. He was born on October 2, 1957.

6.27 False.
St. Louis is not the only NHL franchise to go down in three straight Cup finals. The best of the NHL's six expansion teams in 1967, the Blues only reached the finals because the playoff format pitted them against the other fledgling franchises in earlier rounds. They had little chance of winning the Cup against Montreal in 1968 and 1969 and Boston in 1970. The only other team with a trio of defeats in back-to-back-to-back order is the Toronto Maple Leafs. They lost the Cup finals in 1938 against Chicago, in 1939 to Boston and in 1940 versus New York.

6.28 True.
The stick has been the most common icon on NHL crests since expansion in 1967. At least 10 teams (Pittsburgh, Vancouver, Phoenix, New York Islanders, Washington, Los Angeles, Atlanta, Columbus, Anaheim and San Jose) have used the stick symbol to market the game in new NHL cities. The idea isn't novel. When the old Ottawa Senators franchise moved to St. Louis in 1934 and called themselves the Eagles, their jerseys sported a bald eagle clutching a hockey stick.

6.29 False.
Pelle Lindbergh was killed when his Porsche smashed into a wall in the early morning hours of November 10, 1985. It was a sudden

and tragic end to the 26-year-old Swedish netminder's promising career. Lindbergh had won the Vezina Trophy the previous season and some considered him the NHL's top goalkeeper. In an emotional show of support fans posthumously elected Lindbergh the starting goalie for the Wales Conference team at the 1986 All-Star game.

6.30 True.

Dubbed the "most imaginative moment" of the Queen's Golden Jubilee tour, the sovereign of Canada walked out on a red carpet to centre ice at Vancouver's GM Place, took the ceremonial puck from Wayne Gretzky and dropped it perfectly from her gloved fingers. The puck fell flat on the ice, without bouncing and rolling. It was then scooped up by Canucks captain Markus Naslund, who bowed and handed the puck back to the 76-year-old monarch.

6.31 True.

During the 1995 conference quarterfinals against the San Jose Sharks, the Flames lost their seven-game series 4–3 despite outscoring the Sharks 35–26. Calgary's 35-goal performance in 1995 doesn't top Edmonton's record output of 44 goals and 35 goals during playoff rounds in 1985 and 1983, but neither of those Oilers series went to the seven-game limit.

6.32 False.

Gretzky never scored more than 20 power-play goals in one season. This NHL first belongs to Mario Lemieux. In fact, no goal leader has ever matched Lemieux's level on the man advantage. He netted 31 power-play goals twice, first in 1988–89 when he recorded 85 goals and, later, in 1995–96 with a 69-goal count. In 1988–89, Super Mario also scored an NHL record 13 short-handed goals. One of every two goals scored by Lemieux that season was on a special team.

6.33 False.

Because of Pavel's trade to the New York Rangers and a knee injury that cost Valeri 37 games, the Bure brothers only played together for 26 games with Florida in 2001–02. The Panthers went 5–14–5–2, but the two combined for 18 goals and 20 assists. Pavel's 400th career goal was assisted on by brother Valeri.

6.34 True.

Although only 13 coaches have won the Stanley Cup in their inaugural season, the last four Cup-winning rookies have all come from behind the bench of the Canadiens. Toe Blake won in 1955–56, Claude Ruel in 1968–69, Al MacNeil in 1970–71 and Jean Perron in 1985–86. Jimmy Skinner was the last non-Montreal rookie coach to claim the trophy. Skinner led Detroit to the Cup in 1954–55. The league may be due for another rookie bench boss to win the championship. Only one first-year coach—Jean Perron—has won a Cup since 1970–71.

6.35 False.

Prior to 1969 and the first universal NHL Draft, few top junior prospects were eligible for the draft, most already being under contract to NHL teams through sponsored junior teams. This created some unusual circumstances between 1963—the draft's first year—and 1969. Rick Pagnutti, a defenseman chosen first overall by the Kings in 1967, played 10 years in five pro leagues but never made the NHL. And he was not alone: Claude Gauthier (1964) and Andre Veilleux (1965) were two other first picks whose NHL futures never materialized.

Game 6
OH! CANADA

Some of the smallest towns in Canada are home to hockey's biggest stars. Floral, Saskatchewan, and Thruso, Quebec, are specks on the map, except when you consider their contributions to the sport. In this game match the Hall of Famers in the left column with their Canadian birthplace in the right column.

(*Solutions are on page 121*)

Part 1

1. _____	Bobby Orr	A.	Floral, Saskatchewan
2. _____	Guy Lafleur	B.	Drummondville, Quebec
3. _____	Gordie Howe	C.	Parry Sound, Ontario
4. _____	Ken Dryden	D.	Winnipeg, Manitoba
5. _____	Marcel Dionne	E.	Thurso, Quebec
6. _____	Terry Sawchuk	F.	Hamilton, Ontario

Part 2

1. _____	Bobby Hull	A.	Kitchener, Ontario
2. _____	Dave Keon	B.	Edmonton, Alberta
3. _____	Darryl Sittler	C.	Val Marie, Saskatchewan
4. _____	Bobby Clarke	D.	Noranda, Quebec
5. _____	Johnny Bucyk	E.	Flin Flon, Manitoba
6. _____	Bryan Trottier	F.	Point Anne, Ontario

7
CUP WARRIORS

During the 2003 playoffs Philadelphia coach Ken Hitchcock was asked about fighting through the physical and psychological torture of playoff hockey. "It really comes down to how badly, as a group, you want to keep playing," Hitchcock said. "It's an awful price to pay to continue. I have seen things that I didn't think possible for athletes to do, but once you get to the point you are willing to do it, anything is possible." In this chapter, we champion the indomitable spirit of the Stanley Cup warrior.

(*Answers are on page 104*)

7.1 Who was the first goalie to register two 60-save games in one postseason?
A. Ed Belfour of the Dallas Stars
B. Olaf Kolzig of the Washington Capitals
C. Jean-Sébastien Giguère of the Anaheim Mighty Ducks
D. Martin Brodeur of the New Jersey Devils

7.2 What is the most number of consecutive game-winning goals scored by an NHLer in one playoff series?
A. Two consecutive winning goals
B. Three consecutive winning goals
C. Four consecutive winning goals
D. No player has ever scored consecutive winning goals

7.3 What is the most number of current or former captains on a Stanley Cup-winning team?
A. Six captains
B. Seven captains
C. Eight captains
D. Nine captains

7.4 As of 2003, who holds the record for the most shutouts in one postseason?
A. Martin Brodeur
B. Ed Belfour
C. Patrick Roy
D. Dominik Hasek

7.5 Which former Edmonton Oiler holds the NHL record for the highest career plus-minus in the playoffs?
A. Charlie Huddy
B. Glenn Anderson
C. Jari Kurri
D. Wayne Gretzky

7.6 What is the longest layoff between playoff series by a modern-day team?
A. Six days
B. Eight days
C. 10 days
D. 12 days

7.7 Who was the first goalie to record 50 playoff wins in a career?
A. Turk Broda
B. Glenn Hall
C. Jacques Plante
D. Terry Sawchuk

7.8 Who was the first goalie to record 50 playoff losses in a career?
A. Terry Sawchuk
B. Glenn Hall
C. Gump Worsley
D. Johnny Bower

7.9 Which goalie has taken part in the longest two overtime playoff games in modern-day hockey?
A. Ron Tugnutt
B. Ed Belfour
C. Dominik Hasek
D. Patrick Roy

7.10 Prior to Wayne Gretzky, how many players earned the distinction of winning postseason scoring titles with two different teams?
A. None, Wayne Gretzky was the first
B. Only one player
C. Three players
D. Five players

7.11 How long did Toronto forward Jack McLean have to wait for his Stanley Cup ring after helping the Maple Leafs win the Stanley Cup in 1945?
A. 57 hours
B. 57 days
C. 57 months
D. 57 years

7.12 Prior to brothers Rob and Scott Niedermayer playing opposite each other during the 2003 Stanley Cup finals, when was the last time siblings met during a finals series?
A. 1946
B. 1966
C. 1986
D. It had never happened before

7.13 What is the most number of shots faced by a modern-day goalie in his playoff debut?
A. 44 shots
B. 54 shots
C. 64 shots
D. 74 shots

7.14 Before Anaheim's surprising four-game sweep of the Detroit Red Wings during the preliminary round of the 2003 playoffs, when was the last time the defending Stanley Cup champions lost four straight in the first round?
A. 1932 Montreal vs. New York Rangers
B. 1952 Toronto vs. Detroit
C. 1972 Montreal vs. New York Rangers
D. 1992 Pittsburgh vs. Washington

7.15 Which team first won 10 road games in one playoff year?
A. The 1993 Montreal Canadiens
B. The 1995 New Jersey Devils
C. The 1996 Colorado Avalanche
D. The 1998 Detroit Red Wings

7.16 Who is the only player to score five game-winning goals in one playoff year and not win the Stanley Cup?
A. Bobby Smith
B. Joe Sakic
C. Joe Nieuwendyk
D. Mario Lemieux

7.17 Which third-line winger was the goal-scoring hero for the Montreal Canadiens when they won the Stanley Cup in 1959?
A. Marcel Bonin
B. Claude Provost
C. Don Marshall
D. Phil Goyette

7.18 Which sniper is the only player in NHL history to score every game-winning goal for his team in a best-of-seven playoff series?

A. Joe Sakic of the Colorado Avalanche

B. Mike Bossy of the New York Islanders

C. Mario Lemieux of the Pittsburgh Penguins

D. Jari Kurri of the Edmonton Oilers

7.19 When Toronto's Ed Belfour made 72 saves in a triple-overtime 3–2 win against Philadelphia on April 16, 2003, he came within one save of tying whose modern-day NHL record for most stops in a playoff game?

A. Patrick Roy

B. Dominik Hasek

C. Kelly Hrudey

D. Ron Tugnutt

7.20 In terms of total minutes played, which is the longest playoff series in NHL history?

A. New York Rangers vs. Boston 1939 semifinal

B. New Jersey vs. New York Rangers 1994 Conference final

C. Colorado vs. Detroit 2002 Conference final

D. Toronto vs. Philadelphia 2003 Conference quarterfinal

7.21 Which Stanley Cup champion has travelled the greatest distance with the Stanley Cup?

A. Jere Lehtinen of the Dallas Stars

B. Peter Forsberg of the Colorado Avalanche

C. Pavel Datsyuk of the Detroit Red Wings

D. Alexander Mogilny of the New Jersey Devils

7.22 What is the fewest number of goals allowed in a best-of-seven playoff series? The NHL record was set during the 2003 playoffs
A. No goals
B. One goal
C. Two goals
D. Three goals

7.23 Which sniper owns the NHL record for most career power-play goals in the playoffs?
A. Mike Bossy
B. Mario Lemieux
C. Brett Hull
D. Wayne Gretzky

7.24 During the 2003 playoffs, who became the first player in 70 years to score an overtime goal on a 5-on-3 power play?
A. Joe Sakic of the Colorado Avalanche
B. Vincent Lecavalier of the Tampa Bay Lightning
C. Todd Bertuzzi of the Vancouver Canucks
D. Marian Hossa of the Ottawa Senators

7.25 Which NHL team has suffered the most first round defeats at the hands of Stanley Cup finalists?
A. The New York Rangers
B. The Toronto Maple Leafs
C. The Boston Bruins
D. The Los Angeles Kings

7.26 What is the NHL record for the most consecutive playoff wins by a goalie from the start of a career?
A. Five straight wins
B. Seven straight wins
C. Nine straight wins
D. 11 straight wins

7.27 Which goalie appeared on The Tonight Show with Jay Leno during the 2003 playoffs?
A. Martin Brodeur of the New Jersey Devils
B. Patrick Lalime of the Ottawa Senators
C. Marty Turco of the Dallas Stars
D. Jean-Sébastien Giguère of the Anaheim Mighty Ducks

7.28 What is the most number of different franchises that one general manager has built into Stanley Cup winners?
A. Two different teams
B. Three different teams
C. Four different teams
D. Five different teams

7.29 Which underdog team from the 1986 playoffs is associated with the "Monday Night Miracle?"
A. The St. Louis Blues
B. The Montreal Canadiens
C. The Calgary Flames
D. The New York Rangers

7.30 During the 2003 playoffs New Jersey Devils fans chanted "Marty's better, Marty's better." Which opposition goalie were New Jersey fans slighting in their comparison to Martin Brodeur?
A. Jeff Hackett of the Boston Bruins
B. Nikolai Khabibulin of the Tampa Bay Lightning
C. Patrick Lalime of the Ottawa Senators
D. Jean-Sébastien Giguère of the Anaheim Mighty Ducks

CUP WARRIORS

Answers

7.1 C. Jean-Sébastien Giguère of the Anaheim Mighty Ducks

During the 2003 playoffs Giguère put on a clinic for backstoppers. His Mighty Ducks swept the defending Stanley Cup champion Detroit Red Wings in the first round and then took a commanding 2–0 lead over the Dallas Stars in the next series. In those 18 days Giguère was undefeated, winning all six by one-goal margins. Four games had been decided in overtime. And in two contests the Ducks' playoff rookie kept the fairy tale alive with two 60-save performances: 63 saves in a 2–1 triple-overtime win against Detroit on April 10 and 60 saves in a 4–3 marathon game that took five overtime periods to decide on April 24. The six-foot-one Giguère lost "10 to 15 pounds" in the Dallas game, which turned into the fourth longest overtime game in playoff history. Anaheim's Petr Sykora, who scored the winner at 80:48 of overtime, ate seven Power Bars during the epic battle. Most players from both teams changed gloves, skates, sweaters, socks and T-shirts between periods. Dallas defenseman Sergei Zubov logged 64 minutes of ice time, the most among skaters. Adam Oates, the oldest player in the game at 40, played 39 minutes. At least 10,000 fans were still in the stands when the game ended at 12:36AM Dallas time.

7.2 B. Three consecutive winning goals

During the 2003 playoffs Tampa Bay's Martin St. Louis proved that small players can still play huge roles in the NHL. Never drafted after a promising U.S. college career at the University of Vermont, the five-foot-nine 185-pound winger became just the fourth player in NHL annals to score three straight game winners in one playoff series. After dropping the opening two games against Washington in the first round, the Lightning stormed back and won the next four as St. Louis notched winners in the last three games, including one in triple overtime that gave Tampa a 2–1 victory and their first playoff series win in franchise history. He was also the Lightning's leading scorer in the series with five goals and four assists. "I would like to help out and open some eyes that smaller players can still compete and play hard in this league and have success," said St. Louis. The other players with three straight playoff game winners were all six-feet-two or taller: Boston's Roy Conacher in 1939, Clark Gillies of the Islanders in 1977 and Pittsburgh's Kevin Stevens in 1991.

7.3   B. Seven captains
The most captain-loaded team in NHL history was the 1998–99 Dallas Stars. Dallas GM Bob Gainey, a captain himself with Montreal from 1981 to 1989, built a club boasting seven players who had worn the "C" on other NHL teams: Joe Nieuwendyk (Flames, 1991–1995), Guy Carbonneau (Canadiens, 1988–89), Pat Verbeek (Whalers, 1992–1995), Mike Keane (Canadiens, 1994–1996, Brett Hull (St. Louis, 1992–1997) and Brian Skrudland (Panthers, 1993–1997), in addition to Stars captain Derian Hatcher.

7.4   A. Martin Brodeur
When Dominik Hasek recorded six shutouts on the way to his lone Stanley Cup in 2002, he established a playoff mark that few thought would soon be broken. In NHL history 14 other top-ranked netminders had managed the next-highest mark with four goose-eggs. But just a year later, Brodeur snapped Hasek's benchmark compiling seven zeroes during New Jersey's 23-game march to the 2003 Cup. Brodeur earned shutouts in each playoff round with two zeros against Boston, one against both Tampa Bay and Ottawa and three against Anaheim in the Cup finals where he posted three 3–0 victories, including a shutout in a do-or-die Game 7. It was Brodeur's third Cup.

7.5   A. Charlie Huddy
The dynasty years of the Edmonton Oilers spiked a lot of offensive records in the playoffs. Few records had as many Oilers in the top spots as career plus-minus. Surprisingly, Charlie

Huddy, Edmonton's steady blueliner, heads the list with a plus-93 in 183 playoff games with four teams between 1980–81 and 1996–97. The highest-ranking non-Oiler is Mark Howe with a seventh place plus-51.

HIGHEST CAREER PLUS-MINUS IN THE PLAYOFFS*

Player	GP	Seasons	+/-
Charlie Huddy	183	1981–1997	+93
Jari Kurri	200	1981–1998	+88
Wayne Gretzky	208	1981–1999	+86
Randy Gregg	137	1982–1992	+84
Glenn Anderson	225	1981–1996	+67
Paul Coffey	194	1981–1999	+57
Mark Messier	236	1980–1996	+52
Mark Howe	101	1980–1995	+51

*Current to the 2003 playoff season

7.6   C. 10 days

During Anahiem's remarkable trip to the 2003 Stanley Cup finals, the Mighty Ducks set a record of 10 days downtime after polishing off the Minnesota Wild in the semifinals on May 16 and before their finals match-up against the New Jersey Devils on May 27. Unfortunately history wasn't on Anaheim's side. Their Cup lost represented only the second time a modern-day team failed to win the championship after a rest of seven days or more. Of the last six longest layoffs, the club that was well-rested won five of the six final series. Montreal had nine days off before their Cup-winning series in 1966; the 1984 Edmonton Oilers, the 1952 Detroit Red Wings and the 1949 Toronto Maple Leafs had eight days rest; and the 1999 Buffalo Sabres and 1993 Montreal Canadiens had seven days off.

7.7 A. Turk Broda

Broda was early hockey's best money goalie. He appeared in 21 playoff series and won 15 of them as Toronto racked up five Stanley Cups during his distinguished career from 1937 to 1952. His overtime record was outstanding as well, with 15 wins and eight losses. His 50th playoff victory, a league first, came in 3–1 win against Detroit on April 10, 1949.

7.8 B. Glenn Hall

Only a handful of netminders have had the staying power to withstand 50 playoff defeats. Each share the company of Glenn Hall, who became the NHL's first netminder with a 50-loss record when his St. Louis Blues were defeated 2–1 in double overtime by Philadelphia on April 16, 1968. Hall's Blues were swept by the Montreal Canadiens during the finals, but Hall won the Conn Smythe Trophy as playoff MVP. Mr. Goalie's earned a playoff record of 49 wins and 65 losses between 1956 and 1971. He won one Stanley Cup with Chicago in 1961.

7.9 A. Ron Tugnutt

The two longest games in NHL playoff history took place during the 1930s. On both occasions Lorne Chabot was between the pipes, in 1933 backstopping Toronto in a 1–0 win after 104:46 of overtime and three years later as a Montreal Maroon in a 1–0

LONGEST OVERTIME GAMES IN THE PLAYOFFS*				
Duration	**Winner/Team**	**Loser/Team**	**Score**	**Date**
116:30	N. Smith/Det.	L.Chabot/Mar.	1–0	03.24.1936
104:46	L.Chabot/Tor.	C. Thompson/Bos.	1–0	03.03.1933
92:01	B.Boucher/Phi.	R. Tugnutt/Pit.	2–1	05.04.2000
80:48	J-S. Giguere/Ana.	M. Turco/Dal.	4–3	04.24.2003
79:15	T. Barrasso/Pit.	J. Carey/Was.	3–2	04.24.1996

*Current to the 2003 playoff season

defeat that ended after 116:30 of extra time. Oddly, the two longest overtime games in modern times featured another netminder who dressed in both contests. Ron Tugnutt played in the third longest overtime on May 4, 2000, as a member of the Pittsburgh Penguins and three years later played backup to Marty Turco of the Dallas Stars during that marathon game on April 24, 2003.

7.10 B. Only one player
Hockey statisticians went into overdrive researching the last time someone duplicated Gretzky's playoff feat of scoring titles with two different teams. Only one name came up. Hall of Famer Marty Barry shared the scoring derby lead with Boston in 1930 and then led all playoff performers with Detroit in 1937. A polished stickhandler and policeman with Boston, Barry caught the eye of Detroit GM Jack Adams, who acquired the tough centre in 1935. The Red Wings won successive Stanley Cups with Barry in 1936 and 1937. The Great One claimed five postseason scoring titles with Edmonton and his sixth and last in 1993 as a member of the Los Angeles Kings.

7.11 D. 57 years
Let's hope Maple Leaf fans don't have to wait as long to see their team win another Stanley Cup as McLean waited to receive his Cup ring. McLean played three seasons for Toronto during the 1940s, his last on 1944–45's Cup-winning team. He only received his ring in August 2002 when the Toronto franchise decided to pay tribute to surviving players from championship seasons prior to 1948, when the Maple Leafs first issued team rings to commemorate Cup wins. McLean was one of only nine players honoured. "I haven't been sleeping nights because I've been so excited about this," McLean, 79, said after slipping the ring on his finger for the first time. McLean's name was already engraved on the Cup for the 1945 Cup win.

7.12 A. 1946

The Niedermayers were the first brothers to battle in the Cup final since Boston's Terry Reardon met Montreal's Ken Reardon during the 1946 Cup finals. Although the Niedermayers had gone head-to-head before in the playoffs (in 2000's first round), the family feud still proved a little tough on their mother Carol. "(For) my mom, it might not be an easy situation for her," said Scott. "I guess she probably wishes we both could end up winning, but that's not the case." Ken Reardon won with Montreal in 1946, Scott won his third Cup in 2003 with the Devils.

7.13 C. 64 shots

In a sports story that drew David and Goliath parallels, seventh-place Anaheim beat the heavily favoured defending Stanley Cup champion Detroit Red Wings in four straight games during their conference quarterfinals of the 2003 playoffs. In Game 1 Jean-Sébastien Giguère performed his impression of a wall and stopped a record 63 of 64 shots in the 2–1 triple-overtime victory on April 10, 2003. "It was a great learning experience for me," Giguère said, without a trace of conceit. The turning point of the series was Game 1's first overtime period when Detroit outshot Anaheim 20–4 but failed to score. "If we lose that game, I bet you they crush us," said Ducks coach Mike Babcock. The all-time record for shots on goal by a playoff rookie is held by Normie Smith, who blocked 90 shots in a 1–0 Detroit victory on March 24, 1936.

7.14 B. 1952 Toronto vs. Detroit

In more than a half-century of playoff hockey only two Cup champions have been swept in the first round. Fifty-one years after Detroit swept the defending Cup champion Maple Leafs in the first round of the 1952 playoffs, the Red Wings went down four straight to Anaheim during the preliminary round of 2003. In both series hot rookie netminders stoned the defending Cup champions. In 1952, a kid named Terry Sawchuk broom-handled Toronto. In 2003, Jean-Sébastien Giguère did the honours for the

Mighty Ducks by stopping 165 of 171 shots while posting a stingy 1.24 goals-against average against the high-powered Wings. After being humbled in the series forward Brendan Shanahan put Giguère's play in perspective: "I saw Dominik Hasek in the Olympics in 1998 in a zone. And I haven't seen that before or since until this week with that kid," said Shanahan. According to Las Vegas odds makers the Ducks were 10–1 underdogs to win the series and would have been 150–1 underdogs to sweep.

7.15 B. The 1995 New Jersey Devils

The Devils were one of the NHL's worst road teams during the 1994–95 lockout season, with an uninspired 8–14–2 mark. But New Jersey reversed the trend in the playoffs, going 10–1 on the road and defeating Boston, Pittsburgh, Philadelphia and Detroit to win its first Cup. Coincidentally, New Jersey matched the record of 10 road wins when it claimed its second Cup in 2000.

7.16 A. Bobby Smith

As of 2003, six players in NHL history have scored five-or-more game winners in one postseason. Colorado's Joe Sakic (1996) and Dallas's Joe Nieuwendyk (1999) lead the pack with six game winners, followed by Mike Bossy (1983), Jari Kurri (1987), Mario Lemieux (1992) and Bobby Smith (1991), each notching five winners during their respective playoff years. Smith, however, is the only player among this group without a Cup to show for his efforts, as the Minnesota North Stars fell to the Pittsburgh Penguins in six games during the 1991 finals. Smith did win a Cup in 1986 with Montreal.

7.17 A. Marcel Bonin

With the awesome firepower of Jean Béliveau, Dickie Moore, Bernie Geoffrion and brothers Maurice and Henri Richard on its scoring lines, it's hard to imagine any other Canadien getting sufficient ice time to compete for the playoff scoring race. But Marcel Bonin, a solid third-line winger without a goal in his

25-game playoff career, became just that hero when he subbed for an injured Maurice Richard during the 1959 playoffs. Vaulted onto Montreal's first line with Jean Béliveau and Dickie Moore (until Béliveau himself got injured) the left-shooting winger racked up 10 goals in 11 playoff games and led the Canadiens to their fourth straight Cup. The next highest goal count that season was six goals. Montreal originally picked up Bonin for a song from Boston at the Inter-League Draft in 1957.

7.18   B.   Mike Bossy of the New York Islanders
In the 1983 conference finals between the Islanders and the Boston Bruins, Mike Bossy established an NHL record by scoring all four game winners against Boston. New York moved on to the finals where they man-handled Edmonton in four straight. It was the Islanders' fourth consecutive Cup.

7.19   C.   Kelly Hrudey
Hrudey made a record 73 stops for the New York Islanders in a four-overtime marathon against the Washington Capitals on April 18, 1987. The dramatic 3–2 Game 7 victory in the seventh

MOST SAVES BY A GOALIE IN A PLAYOFF GAME*

Goalie	Team	Opp.	Date	Saves
Kelly Hrudey	NYI	Was.	04.18.1987	73
Ed Belfour	Tor.	Phi.	04.16.2003	72
Ron Tugnutt	Pit.	Phi.	05.05.2000	70
Dominik Hasek	Buf.	N.J.	04.27.1994	70
Bernie Parent	Phi.	St.L.	04.16.1968	63
Patrick Roy	Col.	Fla.	06.10.1996	63
J.S. Giguère	Ana.	Det.	04.10.2003	63

* Current to the 2003 playoff season
* In a game on May 8, 1997, Anaheim netminders faced 70 saves against Detroit. Mikahil Shtlanekov made 38 saves and Guy Hebert made 30.

longest game in NHL history propelled New York into the division finals against Philadelphia, where Hrudey and his exhausted teammates were defeated by the Flyers in seven games.

7.20 A. New York Rangers vs. Boston 1939 semifinal
New York and Boston battled through eight overtime periods in their seven-game death match in 1939. The series included a pair of triple-overtime marathons, the first occuring in Game 1 and the second in Game 7, which was won 2–1 by Boston on Mel Hill's goal at 48:00 of OT. The total series playing time was nine hours, 13 minutes, eight seconds. The Leafs-Flyers seven-game struggle in 2003 ranks second, clocking in at eight hours, 52 minutes, five seconds.

7.21 C. Pavel Datsyuk of the Detroit Red Wings
The Stanley Cup has gone from the bottom of Mario Lemieux's swimming pool to the top of some of Canada's highest mountains, but no player has taken the Cup further than Pavel Datsyuk, who brought it to the Urals city of Yekaterinburg, Russia, where he paraded it on the Continental Divide between Europe and Asia.

7.22 B. One goal
Before the start of the 2003 Cup finals against New Jersey, Anaheim goalie Jean-Sébastien Giguère's work between the pipes was being measured in Conn Smythe Trophy proportions. After disposing of Detroit and Dallas, Giguère shutout the Minnesota Wild in the first three games of the Conference finals. It was only the second time in history a goalie had opened a series with three straight zeros. In Game 4 he allowed just one goal when Andrew Brunette connected at 4:47 of the first period. It ended Giguère's shutout run of 217:44, the fifth-longest streak in NHL history. The 2–1 win earned the Mighty Ducks their first Cup final and the record for the fewest goals in a best-of-seven series.

7.23 C. Brett Hull
Brett Hull broke Mike Bossy's old career mark of 35 power-play goals during the 2002 playoffs, when he scored three times on the man-advantage to take over the lead with 37 goals.

7.24 B. Vincent Lecavalier of the Tampa Bay Lightning
In a playoff series filled with bizarre penalties, including a too-many-men-on-the-ice call during a triple overtime and a four-minute high-sticking penalty on a goalie (Olaf Kolzig), one might expect a penalty-goal combination that only comes along every 70 years. With Washington's Jaromir Jagr (roughing) and Ken Klee (elbowing) in the penalty box, Vincent Lecavalier fired in a rebound at 2:29 of overtime to give the Lightning a 4–3 win against Washington. Lacavalier's winner came in Game 3 of the conference quarterfinals on April 15, 2003. It was the first 5-on-3 playoff overtime goal since April 13, 1933, when New York's Bill Cook scored in the extra period with a two-man advantage against Toronto. (Alex Levinsky and Bill Thoms were the penalized Maple Leafs.) Cook's goal won the Rangers their second Stanley Cup.

7.25 C. The Boston Bruins
Since 1967 post-expansion, a number of NHL clubs have experienced the annual frustration of first round defeats at the hands of the same powerhouse team in their division or conference. Just ask Edmonton, a shoe-string budget team that has drawn rich Dallas routinely and lost five first round series in six match-ups. But what team has had the misfortune of drawing a Cup finalist the most times in the first round? That would be the Bruins, who have endured seven first round exits, three against Montreal and once each against the Minnesota North Stars, New Jersey, Florida and Washington. Toronto and the New York Rangers place second in this category with six first round departures.

7.26 B. Seven straight wins

While Tom Barrasso owns the NHL record for the most consecutive playoff wins (14 straight wins in the 1992 and 1993 playoffs), the leading rookie in this category is Cecil Thompson, who earned five straight wins and the Stanley Cup in 1929 and another two wins to start the 1930 playoffs. During the 2003 playoffs Jean-Sébastien Giguère came within a game of tying Thompson's mark, after winning his first six playoff contests.

7.27 D. Jean-Sébastien Giguère of the Anaheim Mighty Ducks

Giguère, in the middle of a prolonged layoff before the start of the 2003 Cup finals and fast becoming a household name in southern California, guest starred on NBC's *The Tonight Show* on May 23, 2003. During the interview Leno quipped: "You don't look like a hockey guy, you have teeth and everything." Giguère smiled and shot back: "I'm a goalie. I've got a mask." Upon hearing about Giguère's appearance, Cup finals opponent Martin Brodeur of the Devils said: "I wish I could be." Giguère became the first goalie and only the second NHLer to appear on Leno's show. Detroit forward Brendan Shanahan starred after the Red Wings won the Cup in 1997.

7.28 C. Four different teams

Tommy Gorman was one of early hockey's most extraordinary and successful individuals. But despite his triumphs, Gorman still hasn't received his due among the pantheon of builders in NHL history. Conn Symthe and Jack Adams, two of hockey's founding fathers, never won as consistently with as many teams as Gorman. After turning Ottawa into the league's first dynasty with Cups in 1920, 1921 and 1923, he took over the New York Americans, then the Chicago Blackhawks (one Cup in 1934), the Montreal Maroons (one Cup in 1935) and the Montreal Canadiens (two Cups in 1944 and 1946). Gorman won a total of seven Stanley Cups on four different franchises.

7.29 A. The St. Louis Blues

The Montreal Canadiens may have delivered the biggest surprise during the 1986 postseason, but their Stanley Cup championship was just one of the miracles performed that spring. After finishing the regular season just three games over .500, St. Louis fashioned their own string of playoff upsets, missing a trip to the Cup finals by just one game. The Blues first dropped heavily-favoured Minnesota and then knocked off Toronto, both series going the distance. In the conference finals against Calgary, they played underdogs again, inferior to the Flames in almost every position on the ice. Down 3–2 in the series and 5–2 in the score in Game 6, the Blues, just 12 minutes from elimination, pulled off their biggest shocker before 18,000 rabid fans at St. Louis Arena. They scored three times, the last goal with just 1:08 remaining to tie the game 5–5 and force overtime. In the extra period a two-on-one play handed a rebound to Doug Wickenheiser, who potted the winner against Mike Vernon. St. Louis lost a 2–1 heartbreaker to Calgary in Game 7, but their come-from-behind rally in Game 6 captured that wild-ride postseason for the scrappy Blues. For many Blues it was their proudest moment and will forever be remembered as the Monday Night Miracle.

7.30 D. Jean-Sébastien Giguère of the Anaheim Mighty Ducks

Giguère was the story of the 2003 playoffs. Everyone believed it except New Jersey fans, who goaded the Anaheim netminder with chants of "Marty's better, Marty's better" during Game 2 as the Mighty Ducks lost their second straight finals game 3–0. In Anaheim, fans weren't so clever, taunting Brodeur with "Mar-ty, Mar-ty."

Game 7
THE PLAYERS' CHOICE

The Lester B. Pearson Award, which goes to the NHL's outstanding player as selected by the players, is usually bestowed upon big scorers. To date, only two goalies have copped the award in its 31-year history. Mike Liut was the first goalie to win it in 1981 after he led the upstart Blues to a second-place overall finish with a 107-point season. There are 17 family names of Pearson winners listed below. Their names, such as Joe SAKIC, appear in the puzzle horizontally, vertically, diagonally or backwards. After you've circled all 17 names and the word AWARD, read the remaining 19 letters in descending order to spell our unknown Pearson-winning goalie and his team.

(Solutions are on page 121)

Bobby ORR	Jean RATELLE
Sergei FEDOROV	Marcel DIONNE
Phil ESPOSITO	Guy LAFLEUR
Bobby CLARKE	Jarome IGINLA
Jaromir JAGR	Steve YZERMAN
Wayne GRETZKY	Mario LEMIEUX
Mark MESSIER	Brett HULL
Eric LINDROS	Mike LIUT
Joe SAKIC	AWARD

O	R	R	E	L	L	E	T	A	R
L	T	D	V	O	R	O	D	E	F
E	A	I	O	D	I	O	N	N	E
I	K	F	S	M	I	N	N	I	G
X	G	R	L	O	R	G	A	J	R
U	R	I	A	E	P	K	M	H	E
E	E	A	N	L	U	S	R	S	T
I	I	E	L	L	C	R	E	K	Z
M	S	C	I	K	A	S	Z	B	K
E	S	H	U	L	L	U	Y	F	Y
L	E	F	T	D	R	A	W	A	A
L	M	O	S	O	R	D	N	I	L

117

SOLUTIONS TO GAMES

Game 1: Stanley's MVP

As of 2002, only one forward from a losing team has won MVP status in the postseason. It was Reggie Leach of the Philadelphia Flyers in 1976.

Game 2: Defunct Teams

PART 1
1. B. Colorado Rockies
2. C. Philadelphia Quakers
3. G. Montreal Maroons
4. E. Kansas City Scouts
5. A. Cleveland Barons
6. F. Hamilton Tigers
7. D. Atlanta Flames

PART 2
1. G. Brooklyn Americans
2. F. California Golden Seals
3. D. Ottawa Senators
4. A. St. Louis Eagles
5. C. Pittsburgh Pirates
6. B. Minnesota North Stars
7. E. Quebec Nordiques

Game 3: Hockey Crossword

Game 4: Goalie Gunners

1. First goalie to score a goal:
   Billy Smith, New York Islanders, November 28, 1979
2. First goalie to shoot and score a goal:
   Ron Hextall, Philadelphia, December 8, 1987
3. First goalie to score a game-winner:
   Martin Brodeur, New Jersey, February 15, 2000
4. First goalie to score a goal and record a shutout in the same game:
   Damian Rhodes, Ottawa, January 2, 1999
5. First goalie to shoot and score a goal and record a shutout in the same game:
   Jose Theodore, Montreal, January 2, 2001
6. First goalie to score a power-play goal:
   Evgeni Nabokov, San Jose, March 10, 2002
7. First goalie to receive credit for an assist:
   Tiny Thompson, Boston, January 14, 1936
8. First goalie to score 10 points in one season:
   Grant Fuhr, Edmonton, 1983–84
9. First goalie to score three points in one game:
   Jeff Reese, Calgary, February 10, 1993

Game 5: Rearguard Records

Nicklas Lidstrom
Ray Bourque
Doug Wilson
Rob Blake
Phil Housley
Larry Robinson
Gary Suter
Brian Leetch
Steve Duchesne
Serge Savard
Rod Langway

Paul Coffey
Al MacInnis
Chris Pronger
Bobby Orr
Denis Potvin
Larry Murphy
Ian Turnbull
Chris Chelios
Tom Bladon
Doug Harvey
Eddie Shore

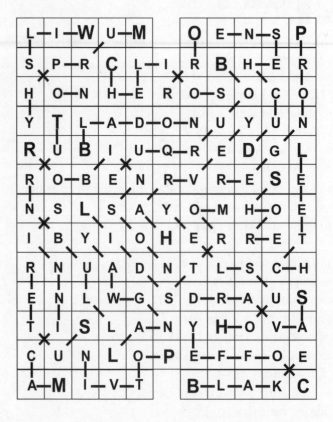

Game 6: Oh! Canada

PART I

1. C. Bobby Orr, Parry Sound, Ontario
2. E. Guy Lafleur, Thurso, Quebec
3. A. Gordie Howe, Floral, Saskatchewan
4. F. Ken Dryden, Hamilton, Ontario
5. B. Marcel Dionne, Drummondville, Quebec
6. D. Terry Sawchuk, Winnipeg, Manitoba

PART 2

1. F. Bobby Hull, Point Anne, Ontario
2. D. Dave Keon, Noranda, Quebec
3. A. Darryl Sittler, Kitchener, Ontario
4. E. Bobby Clarke, Flin Flon, Manitoba
5. B. Johnny Bucyk, Edmonton, Alberta
6. C. Bryan Trottier, Val Marie, Saskatchewan

Game 7: The Players' Choice

In descending order the 19 remaining circled letters spell out:
DOMINIK HASEK BUFFALO. Hasek is the only goalie since Mike Liut to win the Pearson. He did it in back-to-back years, 1997 and 1998.

ACKNOWLEDGMENTS

Thanks to the following publishers and organizations for the use of quoted and statistical material:

- *The Hockey News,* various excerpts. Reprinted by permission of The Hockey News, a division of GTC Transcontinental Publishing, Inc.
- *The National Post.*
- *Total Hockey.* By Dan Diamond and Associates Inc. Published by Total Sports (1998).
- *The Montreal Gazette.*
- *The Globe and Mail.*
- *The Official NHL Guide and Record Book.* Published by Total Sports Canada.
- *The Stick.* By Bruce Dowbiggin. Published by Macfarlane Walter and Ross (2001).
- *The Game I'll Never Forget, 100 Hockey Stars' Stories.* By Chris McDonell. Published by Firefly Books Ltd. (2002).

Care has been taken to trace ownership of copyright material contained in this book. The publishers welcome any information that will enable them to rectify any reference or credit in subsequent editions.

The author gratefully acknowledges the help of Jason Kay and everyone at *The Hockey News;* Gary Meagher and Benny Ercolani of the NHL; Phil Pritchard at the Hockey Hall of Fame; the staff at the McLellan-Redpath Library at McGill University; Rob Sanders, Susan Rana and Chris Labonte at Greystone Books; the many hockey writers, broadcast-journalists, media and Internet organizations who have made the game better through their own work; as well as editor Christine Kondo for her patience, dedication and expertise, fact-checker Kerry Banks for his detail work and love of the game, graphic artist Peter Cocking and puzzle designer Adrian van Vlaardingen for their creativity.